W9-AMU-444

Dream
So Big

Dream So Big

A Parent's Guide to Helping Your Child
Believe &
Achieve

CHRISTOPHER B. PEARMAN
with IAN BLAKE NEWHEM
Foreword by RAVEN-SYMONÉ
Star of the Disney Channel's **That's So Raven**

AVON, MASSACHUSETTS

Published by
Adams Media, a division of F+W Media, Inc.
57 Littlefield Street, Avon, MA 02322. U.S.A.
www.adamsmedia.com

ISBN 10: 1-4405-0402-4
ISBN 13: 978-1-4405-0402-0
eISBN 10: 1-4405-0711-2
eISBN 13: 978-1-4405-0711-3

Printed in the United States of America.

10   9   8   7   6   5   4   3   2   1

Library of Congress Cataloging-in-Publication Data
is available from the publisher.

This publication is designed to provide accurate and authoritative information with regard to the subject matter covered. It is sold with the understanding that the publisher is not engaged in rendering legal, accounting, or other professional advice. If legal advice or other expert assistance is required, the services of a competent professional person should be sought.

—From a *Declaration of Principles* jointly adopted by a
Committee of the American Bar Association and a Committee of
Publishers and Associations

Many of the designations used by manufacturers and sellers to distinguish their product are claimed as trademarks. Where those designations appear in this book and Adams Media was aware of a trademark claim, the designations have been printed with initial capital letters.

This book is available at quantity discounts for bulk purchases.
For information, please call 1-800-289-0963.

Contents

v

A Daughter's Thanks

Parenting matters, and Raven-Symoné is proof of that.

—Bill Cosby

Hi, everyone, it's Raven-Symoné. Up till now only my little brother Blaize and I have been blessed to thrive by my father's parenting principles: his eight "Dream Catchers." But now that I'm taking on the world on my own—and my father's no longer swamped with managing my career—he's decided to share his parenting advice with you. That means you have a chance to do for your child what Christopher and Lydia Pearman—my parents—did for me.

You've probably seen what I've been able to bring about using these Dream Catchers. I'm humbled by what I've accomplished. When I was just three, my dream came true when I got on *The Cosby Show*, the number one show in America. It sounds impossible, but we did it. It made a major impact on millions of people—and it certainly turned our lives upside down. When I was four, my next dream came true when I became the youngest recording artist ever signed to a major label, MCA. Further dreams started to come to fruition in my teens when I starred in movies with some of my idols like Eddie Murphy and Julie Andrews. As a musician, I got to go on tour with 'N Sync. Life can be sweet. And finally, after years of trying, we accomplished my greatest dream: I got my own show, *That's So Raven*, the first sitcom named for an African-American woman. With that I made the history books. Crazy!

You'd be right to assume the odds of all these things occurring were amazingly improbable. But we did it. My family and I know that it took a lot of hard work, long hours, and the blessing of a higher power. But mostly, it took a plan. From the moment I first told my parents that I wanted to be on *The Cosby Show*, my father put that plan to work for us. He probably thought, "Oh, man, what have I gotten myself into?" But he never wavered, and most important, he made sure we were all in it together. Now he's broken this plan down for you into eight Dream Catchers, eight surefire principles for helping your children achieve their dreams, the way he helped me. These Dream Catchers that my father taught me have never failed me. I use them to this day, and every time I do, I know for sure that I'll succeed. And I'm totally confident that your child can succeed, too, whatever they want to achieve.

I know you might be thinking that of course Raven-Symoné would endorse her own dad's book! Well, to keep it real, maybe I would have put a quick quote on the back. But instead I'm writing this foreword, to impress upon you how strongly I believe in these principles, and how strongly I encourage you to give them a shot. Now that you're a parent, what could be more important than making sure your child becomes everything he or she wants to be?

That's not to say it's going to be easy, because it's not. You'll have to do more than just read this book. You'll have to dedicate yourself to putting the Dream Catchers into action, one by one. When I was younger my father concentrated all of his time and energy on helping me accomplish my dreams. Back then I didn't know that he was a man with a plan—I just thought of it as Dad being Dad. However, now that my father has actually written the Dream Catchers out, I understand my life and my success so much better. I'm glad that he was able to put our lessons into words for you and the thousands of people who have asked my family for so many years, "Hey, how did you guys do it?"

The thing about my father is that he puts it all out there on the table. You'll see what I mean as you read. With my father, what you see is what you get. He doesn't pretend to be some kind of guru, and he doesn't believe he did everything right (which he didn't, despite how hard he tried). But he's definitely confident about what he knows, and eloquent in the way he puts it across. I urge you to put his lessons to the test with your kid, and see how far they'll take you both. I think, once you start reading, you're going to find my dad's confidence and enthusiasm contagious.

When I look back now, I remember my father was always focused. Always firm. Always loving. Always thinking about the future. It was kind of like he was always searching for the right way, the most successful way to do things. Make no mistake about it, he was always making sure I watched my p's and q's. I mean always: morning, noon, and night.

Without that love and discipline, I would never have gotten to where I am today. You certainly would not have ever heard of Raven-Symoné.

I'm going to let my dad tell you the rest, but for now, let me just tell you, it's all about balance, learning, and growing. I was taught discipline, hard work, and focus. I was taught professionalism, self-confidence, and honesty. I was taught to listen, to contemplate, to reason, and to learn by example. But I was also taught respect and grace: "Classiness" is what my father would call it. I was taught to aim for the moon, but to keep my feet firmly planted on Earth. And, of course, to keep my head its normal size. I could win an NAACP Image Award one night, and the next morning find myself grounded for not cleaning my room! It makes me laugh to think about it now, but my friends in school (my parents made sure that my Hollywood schedule didn't interrupt my public schooling) called me "Cinderella." Not because I got to attend the ball, but because I had to clean the whole house as penalty for not keeping the birdcage tidy (to this day I don't have a bird). I was definitely not a "celebrity" at home. But I was always a "star" to my father, I suspect from the moment I was born.

An important legacy my father left me is that I grew up not knowing what failure was. When I hit bumps on the road, which of course I did, my dad taught me how to think right, how to fix problems—and he never gave me the option to give up. I get excited when I think about how powerful that kind of confidence and determination can be in your child's life.

Imagine, pouring your heart and soul into helping your child achieve their dreams, and witnessing the amazing results of all of the family's hard work. Imagine your child becoming a genuinely successful adult, someone who loves who they are and what they do. And imagine that your child is genuinely grateful to you—and shows it! That no longer has to be fantasy. I believe that if you put these Dream Catcher principles to work, that beautiful future is well within reach. I believe you will hear from your child the kind of appreciation I'd like to share with my dad right here:

Thanks, Dad, from the bottom of my heart, for catapulting me to the stars. You taught me how to present myself, to love myself, to respect myself, and to believe in myself. I'm so much wiser because of you. I see you in me. And when I look around at the full life we've achieved, I'm touched, thankful, and humbled. You gave me the tools, and someday I will share them with my children. I love you, Dad.

Raven-Symoné
April, 2010

A Father's Promise

My wife Lydia and I had our daughter Raven-Symoné in our mid-twenties, and as young parents, we were scared of making mistakes. I worked at night doing PR for the nightclub industry in Atlanta, and I spent all day with my daughter while Lydia worked as a systems analyst. Raven was a fun and energetic kid who loved her stuffed animals and loved the swings. Like your children, I'm sure, she had enough personality for ten kids. In fact, Raven and I couldn't go out to our beloved Piedmont Park without Raven attracting an unusual number of admirers—crowds, actually. Every day random people asked us if she was in show business, if she was a child model. Perfect strangers insisted that if she wasn't already a star, she should be. After a while, we started to feel that the Universe was trying to tell us something, almost shaking us by the shoulders.

It only made sense. I had dreamed of big things for Raven since before she was even born. I even suggested that we give her, "Two names as one, like a movie star." So I named her "Raven," and Lydia named her "Symoné." We combined the names, knowing that someday the world would know her: "Raven-Symoné."

Raven loved the attention so much that Lydia and I decided to take her to the top modeling agency in Atlanta, Young Faces, Inc. I figured, if they signed her, it was fate, and we had gotten the message right. If not, it wasn't meant to be, and Raven would go on to do other remarkable things with her life. Well, we went in to that agency, and all of the talent scouts gushed, "We *have* to have her." Within months she rose to the top of the Atlanta market. She was poised, professional, attentive, and definitely talented—all so unusual for a toddler. People in the neighborhood even started to recognize Raven from her ads for local stores. We watched in amazement as Raven absolutely conquered all the aspects of child modeling.

If you ask her, she would say the best part of modeling was when she could actually see herself in the paper on Sundays, in pictures almost as big as she was. As parents, we believed the most important part was that she enjoyed it, she found her efforts rewarding, and she blossomed. The spotlight and even the hard work seemed to fill some essential need in her. She would do a shoot, earn some money, and buy a Barbie or some game, all the while basking in the attention for something she earned. Of course, Grandma, well, she loved all those newspaper photos framed on her walls.

Belief in a Dream

I began to realize that I had helped this amazing flight to the stars get off the ground. I had believed in Raven, I had pictured many wonderful triumphs for her, I had encouraged her in all pursuits, and refused to admit the possibility of mediocrity. All that whispering to baby Rae-Rae—"You're the greatest, you're a star"—had somehow gotten a foothold insider her, and, bless her, she was on her way now—there was no stopping her journey.

But nothing prepared us for that Thursday night that Raven lay on her belly in front of *The Cosby Show*, her tiny feet waving in the air in pink socks and pajamas. Like most of America, we always watched Cosby. It was the highest rated show on television at the time—number one every year for the previous four years. With Raven, Cosby was a bit of an obsession, really, as he had been for me when I was young watching his early TV work. From the sofa behind her we watched her, mesmerized by the Huxtable family. We knew that she loved Rudy, the beautiful, talented little girl played by Keshia Knight Pulliam. What we didn't know yet was that as she watched, little Raven (empowered by her modeling accomplishments and our constant encouragement) was watering the tiny seed of a dream in her head, and it was already taking root. She was nurturing a powerful hope that, once spoken, would change all our lives forever, propelling us all in a direction even a dreamer like me could never have imagined. Suddenly, little Rae-Rae turned to us and declared, "You know, I can do what Rudy does. *I want to be on that show.*" What an amazing moment, frozen in time for me.

First, let me say that right away that I *knew* she was right. I knew she could do it. But I tempered it with a dose of reality. There's a big difference between modeling for shopping malls in the *Journal-Constitution* and acting on one of the most popular shows in the world—a show that didn't have a role for her, a show that had never even heard of her! But I can honestly say it never struck us to humor her with platitudes, or worse, to respond, "C'mon now, girl, that's impossible." Instead, Lydia and I shared a look that said: There's no reason to believe she *can't* do it. And then my first thought was, now, how in the hell do we meet Bill Cosby?

You see I knew—I just *knew*—that Cosby was the ticket. I knew that all that time in my youth I'd watched the Cos, and dreamed of someday meeting him, had all come to this. This mission. It sounds ridiculous, of course, but I knew that if Bill Cosby could somehow meet Raven-Symoné, he'd change his show, somehow create a role for, cast her, and she'd be a huge hit. You can call me overconfident.

A Dream in Action

So that summer, my wife Lydia and I pulled up stakes in Atlanta to pursue our daughter's dream of landing a role on *The Cosby Show*. We like to say we've seen New York from the bottom up. Life in that big, unforgiving city was tough in the beginning, just like in the movies. We lived in a pay-by-the-night motel in Secaucus, New Jersey, between the Meadowlands and the Jersey Turnpike. In the morning, we took the PATH train into Manhattan. It was 100 degrees. Of course we were never neglectful, but beyond the basic necessities (hot dogs from the Exxon station beside the motel), there were few luxuries. If it was a really good day, we could afford a donut for little Rae-Rae in the evening after all our auditions and casting calls.

We knew nobody in New York—certainly not Bill Cosby, the biggest TV star in America! But Raven started to get gigs: She did spots for Jell-O, Fisher Price, Ritz Crackers, and Cool Whip. That said, we were still a long way away from the big leagues. One day while we were coming from an audition, we saw the sign for the William Morris Agency. Since we were going for broke anyway, we decided to give the biggest talent agency in the world a shot. It was one of those classic New York moments. You know, "If you can make it there, you'll make it anywhere!" So we wheeled Raven into the lobby, and I confidently asked the receptionist, "Excuse me, is there someone we can speak to about this talented young girl?"

The receptionist shot us a look that said it all. "And YOU are . . . ?"

I persisted: "I'm the father of Raven-Symoné, who's got big dreams."

Needless to say, we didn't get past the lobby of William Morris.

A Healthy Dose of "I Think I Can!"

As young parents, of course we often worried whether we were doing the right thing. We even fought about it on occasion. To be honest, there were times we had to overcome a strong desire to pack it in, you know, and take an easier road.

Wouldn't it have been better for everyone—even Raven—to go back to Atlanta, to our family, our support, our safety net? Together we decided that as long as Raven wanted this, we'd help her get it. Truth is, if Raven had ever complained, if any of us had decided it wasn't worth it—or even wavered for a moment—we might have turned around and gone back to Georgia. Boy, my in-laws sure would have been relieved.

But our girl could not be swayed. When we looked down and saw Rae-Rae in her carriage, beaming, she'd say, "Mama, Daddy, I'm gonna be like Rudy!" Declarations like that traveled from Raven's heart directly into mine. Sometimes you learn the most important lessons from your children. I mean, just like Raven, I absolutely knew it in the fiber of my being. There was nothing I wouldn't have done to make sure that our daughter's dreams came true. Our mutual enthusiasms fed off each other. We went on audition after audition, unwilling to give up. Our little family was totally focused on Raven's dream: We were like three people with one shared goal, with one consciousness even. We were so sure we'd get there that the bumpy ride didn't even bother us most of the time. And you know what? Each step on that journey, no matter how small, was bringing us closer into Bill Cosby's orbit.

A year later, after much striving, Raven landed an audition for a Bill Cosby movie called *Ghost Dad*. Later on, in "Dream Catcher One: Pay Attention," I'll tell you what it meant to me to finally meet Bill Cosby. For now, though, I'll tell you what it meant to Raven. She was too young for the film part, but Cosby loved her so much that he asked the writers of his television show to create a role for her. The "impossible" dream became a reality. We had never doubted it.

And the rest is history. My daughter Raven-Symoné became a cast member on *The Cosby Show*. Costarring, in a role they wrote just for her. (We found out later that the producers intended to keep her on for just four episodes, but she did so well, and the audience response was so positive, they kept her on.) At the time, some critics said Raven saved *The Cosby Show*. And after her three incredible seasons on *Cosby*, after America fell in love with little "Olivia Kendall," Norman Brokaw, the president of the William Morris Agency, not only let us past the lobby of his offices, he became Raven's agent.

Our daughter Raven would never again have to worry about anyone barring her entry to any room, anywhere.

That great sense of accomplishment, relief, and exhilaration we felt as parents . . . it's impossible to put that into words. And it was an indelible lesson for Raven. She told us her dream, and we made it happen, together. Success snowballed, and so many more victories followed. Raven did other successful TV shows and movies. She acted with Eddie Murphy and Julie Andrews and other megastars. She was the youngest recording artist ever signed to a major label. She eventually got her own show, *That's So Raven*, and was the first African-American girl to have a sitcom named for her. She started to serve as the executive producer. And before she was twenty-one, our little girl had created a $400 million empire for Disney! Most important, she did it all with class, self-respect, and joy.

Applying the Dream Catcher Principles

After twenty years of fathering and managing Raven (as well as rearing her wonderful younger brother, Blaize)—often with certainty, but sometimes through trial and error—I learned a lot. And when Raven became independent a few years ago, I started to think about the amazing life we'd embarked on together. With some unaccustomed free time, I began a spiritual journey and did some traveling. I read a lot, and spoke with so many great men and women with inspiring and amazing families. I sought connections to what I'd accomplished with Raven, and began to think deeply about what I'd learned. Finally, I met a wonderful writer named Ian Blake Newhem, who helped me get my ideas into a book form.

It's my greatest wish that you, too, can experience the bliss that comes from reflecting on your children's success, from knowing that they, too, can be inspired to dream and taught the tools to achieve and live out their wildest dreams.

In this book, I will share with you more aspects of our journey, but this is not Raven's story, nor mine. It's your children's, and yours. My goal for this book is to share the Dream Catchers my wife and I employed to help our child realize astounding success. I know that if you had the right tools at your disposal, you could do the same. Then you, too, could bask in the satisfaction that comes from sitting back and watching your children achieve their dreams and beyond.

But let me be clear up front: I'm not a child psychologist—and I certainly am not a perfect parent. I'm not a philosopher or a preacher, either. And you'll notice I'm not a fancy academic with a million-dollar vocabulary and a string of degrees. I started out like you, probably, just a normal, average parent in every way. But, step by step and day by day, my family succeeded at something remarkable and meaningful, something for which I think we are all justifiably proud. As the father and former longtime manager of one of America's favorite young stars, a special little girl who became a lovely, thriving young woman, I hope you'll lend me your trust and give my ideas a try. I believe strongly that you can use the same eight Dream Catchers to make your children's dreams come true.

Hundreds of times I've heard parents lament, "If I only knew then what I know now." There's always a stabbing regret and pain behind that statement, even when it's said lightheartedly. I definitely felt that sometimes, and once in a while, I still do. But looking back now, with 20/20 hindsight, I can see clearly the keys to our triumphs, and just as vividly I can see the pitfalls and mistakes. I know it might sound corny, but I feel a calling to help save parents like me from needless anxiety, from blind alleys, and from the guilt and self-recrimination that so often come with parenting. My greatest dream for this book is that it will heighten your confidence and give you practical tools to help your children find themselves, grow, flourish, hope, and exceed their wildest dreams.

Although it contains a few stories of "stardom," this is not a book about being a stage parent, nor about finding agents and managers, and choosing roles. This is a how-to book about guiding *your* children toward success and fulfillment in any endeavor—whether in Hollywood, or Anytown, USA.

I can't you give a perfect roadmap, of course, but I can put up some guideposts, show you how to swerve around the roadblocks, and even brush away the weeds so you can appreciate the milestones. But I intend to leave you in the driver's seat for this rewarding, heart-pounding, all-too-fast ride that is your children's dreams. So buckle up, and let's hit the road!

Why Dream Catchers?

From the time I was a kid I've been fascinated by Native American culture and mythology, especially the Dream Catcher symbol. According to the ancient custom, parents placed a Dream Catcher above the bed of their child in order to filter out the bad dreams and allow only good, affirmative dreams to pass through the web. Good dreams filter through feathers into the soul of the sleeping child. And bad dreams get tangled in the web—the way spiders trap flies—and disappear by morning. The Native Americans of North America made Dream Catchers from hoops made of willow or grapevine, with sinew (animal tendons) or suede strands woven into that symbolic spider web. They used these fragile, organic materials in order for them to eventually dry out and collapse naturally as their children grew into adulthood, when they could sort out the positive from the negative themselves. So wise and lovely, that custom.

When it came time for Lydia and me to devise our doctrines for raising our children to reach their full potential, I hadn't quite solidified the Dream Catcher analogy, but it's so clear to me now in retrospect. I see it now, and it's beautiful: We created principles that acted as Dream Catchers for our children, while they were asleep and awake. The eight Dream Catchers I present in his book are spiritual and practical principles that will filter the negativity of the world, and allow only encouragement and optimism to pass through into your children's consciousness. By incorporating these Dream Catchers into your family's life at home, you will witness your children overcome so-called challenges and limitations that might otherwise bury them.

It's a high-tech, fast-as-lightning, "ADD" environment our kids are growing up in today. They are inundated daily with a level of sensory overload that would send Huck Finn or the kids from *Little House on the Prairie* spinning, yet they're still starved for meaning and purpose and individuality, just as children have always been. Maybe this is one of the reasons there are so many kids suffering depression and other mental challenges nowadays. I hope and believe that these eight Dream Catchers are essential for grounding, stabilizing, and decompressing our kids today. They are designed not as "rules" to adhere to like military commands, but guidelines given in the spirit of sharing. The Dream Catchers will promote freedom for your children to dream without limitations. Using them, the nightmares that plague and stupefy some children will get tangled in the webs you create for them, where those monsters will find themselves quietly devoured in the night.

And just like real Dream Catchers, whose wood and sinew web begins to wear out naturally as the child passes into adulthood, these eight Dream Catchers will prepare your children to develop strong, independent, and unique personalities. As your children grow into adulthood, you can slowly back away, as I did with Raven, knowing that you have instilled in them a spirit of courage and perseverance. You'll be certain, as I was, that by the time the Dream Catchers deteriorate (by the time your children are too old for you to manage their lives using these principles), the principles will be wholly internalized, as much a part of your children's consciousness and unconscious as their sense of humor or even their breathing. And your job will be done. You can sit back and enjoy their joy and success.

Start the Dream Catcher Journey

As you begin this journey, pay attention to your children's expression of their dreams. Encourage them, listen, and discuss their limitless future. Where do they want to go? What do they want to achieve? How do they picture their future? All dreams begin with imagination, so remember to foster an unlimited imagination in your children. Don't always try to temper imagination with "reality," and beware imposing your own insecurities, fears, and limits on your children. Imagine if President Barack Obama's mother had told him he couldn't ever become all he wanted to become. I hope that as you read this book, any skepticism you might still have will melt away. But be warned, you might get some bumps and bruises along the way. As the Russian proverb says, "The toe of the stargazer is often stubbed."

Get Your Own House in Order

In my youth I stressed freedom, and in my old age I stress order. I have made the great discovery that liberty is a product of order.

—Will Durant, American writer, historian, and philosopher

I n order to take on the task of dedicating yourself to your children's goals, please consider the following common-sense advice in the form of a careful self-inventory to ensure you're ready. The message is: *It helps to sort out yourself first, before you can begin to manage your children's lives.* And that's exciting news, because if you're anything like me, some self-improvement is always helpful. There are several key obstacles most parents need help to overcome, including: the fear of rejection, the fear of failure, and the potential for falling short or even resenting your children if you're more committed to fulfilling your own dreams than theirs.

A Healthy You Is Vital to Your Children's Success

If you're anything like I was as a new parent, you're a nervous wreck. Even if you're not a new parent, you might still suffer the anxiety common to all parents.

Does This Sound Like You?

- You don't know if you're up to the task of raising children.
- You don't know whether you'll ever be "ready."
- Your children are special, but you don't know how to make things "happen" for them.
- You're nervous about inflicting your own insecurities and fears on your children.
- You worry about the impact your words and actions might have on your children.
- You want more for your children than what you had as a child, or currently have.
- You're afraid that you don't know what your children really want.
- You haven't gotten it right before, so maybe it's too late now.
- You're especially concerned about how good a role model you are.

If you agreed with a couple of these statements, congratulations—you're a parent, and a conscientious one, at that. I promise you that the Dream Catcher principles will greatly ease your anxieties—but you'll have to "sort yourself out" first.

Good News!

Worrying about your parenting skills means you're normal. It's only bad news if you allow your own fears and insecurities to stymie the enormous potential you have to foster your children's dreams, to influence their self-esteem, their happiness, and the practical facts of their future. To be frank, before you embark on these principles to guide your children toward dream fulfillment, you've got to sort out yourself first. If that seems like a daunting proposal, don't worry: I've got some suggestions for you to make it manageable and even rewarding. If you're still wondering why you matter in the process of your children's dreams coming true, consider this: Have you ever heard the flight attendant on a plane announce that if you're traveling with a small child you should "Secure your own oxygen mask before securing your child's"? Ever thought about that? While at first blush it seems counterintuitive, there's a whole lot of wisdom in those instructions. In an emergency at 30,000 feet, your children need you breathing, to assist with their ongoing needs. The same principle applies on the ground.

Cognitive psychologists have determined that a child builds a "self"—either a healthy and balanced one, or an unhealthy and unbalanced one—based on their answers to four imperative questions:

Questions Children Ask to Form a "Self"
1. Are the people around me safe or dangerous?
2. Is the world fundamentally good or bad?
3. Does my life have a meaning—or no meaning?
4. Am I a good person—or bad?

Now, guess where children find answers to those critical questions. That's right—from you, their parent. Sometimes the answers come in an obvious and transparent form, such as when you lean into a child's crib and assure them they are loved and protected. But more often, the answers come more subtly, through the model you provide in your daily life, through the messages you send them every day, day after day, by your actions and behaviors. The point is, the answers necessary for children to build a strong "self" do not come from magical leprechauns or from their own DNA. They come from you. So you have to *provide* a sense of safety, *be* good, *insist* on meaning, and *impart* a strong sense of worthiness in your children. In fact, that's pretty much what we signed up for when we chose this job as parent. But it's exceedingly hard to do all that when your own answers to those questions are unclear.

So first and foremost, you'll have to conduct an honest self-inventory. You'll learn as we proceed into the Dream Catcher principles that we can't influence big things in life without a healthy level of awareness. We become aware by searching ourselves, asking challenging, sometimes uncomfortable questions, then answering honestly. And if you're intending to guide your children into a state of self-awareness, you're going to first have to become aware yourself. It doesn't matter when you begin this process—you might have an infant in the cradle or a teenager camped out in the attic with headphones—it's never too late to start, and it's always healthy and gratifying. This book is about your role in facilitating your children's dreams, but I hope as an ancillary benefit, you might feel yourself improved and better equipped to deal with your own life.

Below I've outlined some of the tough questions you'll need to ask yourself and resolve before you commit to the eight Dream Catcher principles.

The Scary Questions
- Are you willing to synthesize your dreams with your children's?
- Are you willing to make the time?
- Are you willing to stop making excuses?
- Are you willing to believe that anything is possible?

Are You Willing to Synthesize Your Dreams with Your Children's?

Ask yourself before anything else, where are you? I mean in your life. To what extent have you achieved your own dreams? What faraway accomplishments still haunt you? Did you always want to be famous for swimming the length of the Hudson? Is your life's ambition to work for yourself as a cabinet builder, or to climb the world's 100 highest peaks without oxygen? Well, of course you can be an excellent parent, raising healthy and balanced kids, even while you're devoted to your own mission and goals. This is especially true if you have a spouse devoted to your child. Let me be clear: I'm not saying that if you're pursuing your own dreams, you can't be devoted to your children's dreams. This is not an all-or-nothing proposition. As a matter of fact, to a certain extent, pursuing and accomplishing *your* goals provides a valuable model for your children to see and to learn from. So you might consider fulfilling those dreams, or versions of them, as prerequisites to helping your children fulfill theirs.

But I *am* saying there's a hard truth to these upcoming Dream Catcher principles: In order to make your children's dreams come true, you, as parent and guide, must be ready not to put your dreams second, but to *synthesize* your dreams with theirs. For many, this is one of those open secrets about parenting. If there's major competition between your efforts in pursuit of your own stuff, and helping them achieve theirs, you can bet somebody's going to lose. If your goals are in competition with your children's, you will resent the time and effort you lose for your own important pursuits, and you might even (heaven forbid) resent your child for distracting you from your own mission.

Even if you manage to escape resentment, you still can't expect impressive results for your children unless you give yourself over *as much as possible* to your children's dreams. So regardless of how devotedly you follow your own dreams, you mustn't neglect those of your children. All parents understand what the reality is: Your personal ambitions need to take a backseat to a certain extent during your child's formative years, so that you can devote your best time and energy (your attention) to them.

Look, plenty of children wind up doing great, even when they haven't had the most attentive parents. Some children simply seek a higher level, even when they lack a strong foundation. Some overcome tremendous odds with little or no help from their parents—and often with no parents at all.

You might even be one of those people who "made it" despite less-than-ideal circumstances. But now that you're a parent, if you can stack the odds in favor of your children's success, why wouldn't you? In the worst-case scenario, if you don't focus on your children's dreams, one day you might suffer regret.

Some would argue that putting your children second is a surefire way to stunt their growth and potential—not to mention your relationship—and you will undoubtedly be sorry that you were not there for them as much as they needed you. Perhaps that's overly dramatic. But what a tragedy if it's true. Or even if your children only *perceive* that it's true. So why take the chance? Why not seize the opportunity now to do what your heart and your instinct tells you, and be there for your children as their biggest Dream Catcher, holding their hand on their journey toward their dreams?

Sounds Like Too Much to Ask?

You were hoping I'd tell you that you could make your children's wildest dreams come true with minimal effort and "no money down"? Sorry. From my experience, it's much more likely they need you, and need you all the way. You're the adult, the mature one, the experienced one, the wise one. They need you to help them sort out:

- Who they are
- What the world is telling them
- What they want out of life

- How to prioritize things
- How to think straight about their dreams and themselves
- How to believe in themselves
- How to tap into the resources that can help them
- What to do when they encounter resistance
- How to deal with fear and disappointment
- How to behave along the way, and once they achieve their dreams

I know it all sounds like a tall and intimidating order. But let me give you four pieces of wonderful news to ease your worry. . . .

Finally Finding Out Who You Are Can Be a Life-Changer

It's probably clear to you by now that you'll need to formulate your own answers to those critical questions above before you can be optimally useful to your children in helping them answer for themselves. This is good news because many of us have not done the kind of self-improvement that we deserve (and most of us probably need). So here's permission to think about yourself, to figure out what you're all about. You can do this alone, in a quiet place, over the course of a few weekend mornings, for example, or before anyone else gets up. Or maybe you could go on some long hikes or drives, or walk on the beach, or even take your dog out for a series of a lengthy walks, during which you ponder those questions, and get straight with yourself. You could even do those exercises with a therapist if you like. Or an encouraging spouse or friend. If you like to write, then keep a journal with your answers.

It's important to remember that the goal here is not to relive past agonies, humiliations, and defeats. The point is to clarify for yourself who you are and what makes you tick. If there's room for improvement—if, for example, you'd prefer not to give up on things so easily—then acknowledge that, commit to working on it, and move on. Make these self-inventories a regular practice and they will eventually become habit. You will benefit greatly in your own life—and you'll be a more valuable resource for your children as you escort them through their own journey.

A Dream Is a Wish Your Child Makes

Hearing your children's dreams announced to the world, really hearing them—and seeing the hope and desire in their eyes as they plead with you as Raven pleaded with me—will change you. Your previous objectives will seem petty and self-ish. You will realize, *Ah, yes—that's why I had a kid!* In short, and to borrow an idea from Disney, *your* dream is a wish *your child* makes. In other words, your child's dreams meld with your own. Your children's success *becomes* your greatest dream, and it seems that nothing else matters. And soon, if you're truly blessed, their greatness dwarfs your own stuff. Their dreams really do subsume your own, become your own, and you're thrilled about it, not resentful. It's not that you're coming in "second." You're both together, both "first." If you're skeptical about this, I promise you it happened not only to me, but to the hundreds and maybe thousands of parents of exceptional children I've encountered from Hollywood to neighborhoods everywhere that look just like yours. Personally, I can tell you that whenever people ask me whether I put my own dreams "on hold" for Raven, my reply is immediate: *No, sir. We shared the dream. Together, we were the dream.* And it never felt like a sacrifice.

You Will Rise

This might surprise you, but I promise you will be able to rise to the level of your children's aspirations, just as I did. You likely won't have to dedicate twenty years and 100 percent of your energy to this fulfillment. But you can't even imagine what you are capable of when it comes to your children. When you look at your progeny and think, *It's you and me kid, together*, you can achieve so much more than either one of you could on your own. And you will be proud of what you never even expected you could help your children accomplish.

You Will Have Your Time, Too

There will always be time for you. Your children are always your children, but you have a relatively short window to be everything to and for them. Take advantage of this short amount of time, because before you know it, your children will be all grown up and they won't need you in that way anymore. Even after I dedicated two decades to Raven, there's still plenty of time now for me to pursue my own goals. And now I'm doing it freely, knowing I'm not selling my children short.

Still Not Sure You Can Commit?

If it's not immediately obvious to you that your bliss will come when you fully invest in your children's dreams, I urge you to try this: First, pay careful attention to your children, starting today, in a more intense way, and see if you can discern what their souls are reaching for. Look in their eyes, listen to them, hold their hand, and ask some gentle, probing questions to unlock their dreams.

Ask Your Kids These Questions
- What do you love to do?
- What would you do all day long if you could?
- What's your greatest, most secret, and "impossible" dream?
- How do you picture the "perfect" future for yourself?

Do this for a few days, maybe a few weeks. Really pay attention, without distractions.

Then spend some quality time alone. Be by yourself for at least a few hours, maybe a whole weekend, if that's possible. And while you're sequestered, search your own soul, your mind, your spirit, your conscience, for an answer. If, like me, you find your dream is to see your children's wishes come true (and to be hands-on and involved with that achievement), then you're ready to make their dreams a top priority.

Once you do that, concede that you will have to prioritize and make what might at first seem like some sacrifices. That's okay. Live with it. Accept it. You'll be gaining so much more than you might at first perceive you'll be giving up. When, later, you start building a plan for your children's dream fulfillment, you can work in some appropriate time for yourself, to continue pursuing your own dreams, too.

Are You Willing to Make the Time?

Setting priorities means that you necessarily have to bump some things to the bottom of your list. Decide which things in life just aren't important, and then simply stop doing them. While it's valuable to decompress at times, imagine how many more important things you could accomplish—and how much time you would have—if you simply bumped these top three time-wasters down, or off of the list entirely: surfing the Internet, watching mindless TV, and responding (or sending out) unnecessary e-mails. All these things can wait.

For those tasks you really must take care of, consider "batching" them together during certain predetermined periods of the day. For example, you might respond to all your e-mails, texts, and phone messages only between 3 and 4 P.M., and you can train all your correspondents that this is the way you do things.

The Time Management and Life Balance Miracle

Hard to determine what's really important and what's a time-waster? Use the 80/20 Principle. The whole point of the 80/20 Principle is to maximize the time you have left, after all the time you have to spend on those things you must do, like working to make ends meet. The idea is that most things (80 percent) fall in the "trivial" category, and the valuable things fall in the "vital" category (20 percent). It's in prioritizing and time management where the 80/20 Principle can be your best friend. Only a small portion of all the things we do—about 20 percent—actually matters. By "matters," I mean gets us closer to our ultimate goal, our dream, our "mission" in life. Those things are considered "valuable" that move us toward our dreams. That means the other 80 percent of everything you do (*most* of what you do) doesn't have as much *value*, because it doesn't propel you toward your goals or dreams. For example, let's say you set as an important goal to help your children study for the county spelling bee. The moment you do that, only those things you do to support that goal will have value. So schmoozing with a buddy at the deli, baking peach cobbler, staying late at work, learning a new language—enjoyable as these things might seem at the time—don't *need* to be done. None of these things, the 80 percent of activities that occupy your time, will help get your children on that podium remembering how to spell *onomatopoeia*. So you might have only a few hours a week after all your obligations are complete, but you can optimize those few hours.

The great part about employing the 80/20 Principle is that once you've determined what's among the "vital few" items on your to-do list, you seldom feel conflicted about back-burnering all the other things—you're just riding on the wave that's moving rapidly toward your goal.

80/20 Your Own Goals

If you 80/20 the things that you want to achieve in your own life, you'll find that you'll have freed up enormous time and energy that can be filled by helping your children with theirs. The point is that there's always more time. Find it by 80/20-ing everything in your life, then use the newfound time and energy you have for this important goal: helping your children achieve their dreams. However much time you have, devote it seriously and smartly to what matters: your children, and where they want to take their lives.

Are You Willing to Stop Making Excuses?

I understand that life can be hard for those of us who aren't spectacularly wealthy. I get that you have to work, and you probably have lots of obligations (possibly including caring for you own aging parents). In short, I know you probably have lots of other stuff going on in your life, besides helping your children pursue their dreams. But I encourage you not to get in the habit of using your responsibilities as *excuses* for not heeding the call of your children's dreams.

I'm sympathetic: I know that you don't intend to make "excuses" for what you know is important—your children achieving all they set out to achieve. I don't mean to sound harsh, especially as I know personally what it's like to juggle all the duties, worries, and insecurities that come with adulthood. When you add children on top of all that, it can seem like the hardest thing in the world. But it is important here for me to "keep it real." Some of us have a tendency to fall into unproductive and unhealthy ways of thinking, and sometimes it takes some tough love advice to knock you out of that. Only you will truly know whether or not you're making excuses.

If you are, you can overcome them. Once you discover your children's talents, and understand the extent of their dreams, you'll need to throw as many resources at your child as possible, *within your means*. So let's review your "means": time, money, and education.

No Time

This is a big challenge, and I've already covered some techniques for it in the 80/20 section. But here I want to address attitudes about time, and offer some practical counsel. Time is finite, so you have to choose what you will do with it. If you have time obligations in your day (almost all of us do: They call it "work") then it gets even more limited. But still you can *choose* what do with the time you have left. Of course you can work from 8:00 to 5:00 or even beyond, but then you can choose to spend a couple of hours cultivating your children's dreams. Choose to do that instead of watching TV or quilting or puttering around your workshop when you get home. Or if you must work Monday to Friday, you can still decide to spend most weekends working on your children's dreams—instead of golfing or fishing or antiquing (or napping). This is a rule of the Universe worth memorizing: *Your children are going to get out of life what you put into them.* This is as true for time as for any of your other resources. At the end of the day, if you do a little, you're going to get a little. If you do a lot, you'll likely reap a lot.

Can't find the time? okay, let's examine that. You know you have responsibilities now as a parent. You know your time— even small amounts of your time—is awesomely valuable to your children. And you know the consequences of "can't find the time," if that attitude persists for long enough, could be devastating.

You don't need huge amounts of money or some "privilege" to make these Dream Catchers work. But you *do* need some time—it's perhaps the most valuable resource in your arsenal. It's truly astounding what a couple of quality hours a day can do for children's development. Case study after case study backs up this profound truth. You can even start small. Just an hour a day, 365 hours a year, is equivalent to more than nine work weeks of support. How much would your children's singing or gymnastics or soccer skills improve with nine full weeks of training with you as coach? How much closer would your children be to publishing their first poem, or giving their first piano recital, or raising money for a meaningful charity, with nine solid weeks of dedication from you? You won't know until you try it, but you can probably predict. They'd be closer. Now I'm not saying you should spend only an hour a day. If you have more time— spend more time, of course. I certainly spent a lot more than an hour a day helping Raven get where she wanted to go. The good news is that throwing quality time at a problem is far more beneficial in my experience than throwing money at it.

No Money
Been there. In the winter of 1986, when Raven was barely a year old, we were living in a two-bedroom apartment in Atlanta. We weren't dirt poor—we just had some big bills. I was managing PR for some local nightclubs, and Lydia was

in IT. We were a typical young couple striving. Something had shifted when it hit us that we were going to have a child. We needed to pay for diapers, clothing, insurance, medical stuff, everything. I took on a second job delivering pizza just to make ends meet, but there was always too much month left at the end of the money. We wondered how other people manage it, and how some people—that select few—make extraordinary things happen financially. Some people might think, "Well, all we have to do is keep pressing on, keep plugging away, and it'll all work out." But that didn't seem like a safe enough bet for me. I kept thinking, *Instead of continuing to delivering pizza, maybe I ought to go for the lottery, you know, the jackpot.*

But in the meantime, the bills were piling up. Then one of our famous ice storms hit. Planes were sliding off the runway at Hartsfield, and roads were closed. After dinner, our heat suddenly went out. I frantically called the power company, thinking the weather might have somehow knocked out the heat. But they told me they'd *shut off* our heat. They said we hadn't paid the bill. Well, we scrambled around, and couldn't even find the bill, no less a "past due" notice. We pleaded with them. I remember actually begging, saying, "I have a little baby daughter. She could die in this cold!" I told them I would come down right away and pay. And the woman on the other end of the line said, "We can't help you."

It was a definite low point. There's nothing like your wife looking over at you, holding your firstborn, and you can see their breath, and practically read your wife's mind. It's times like this you realize how vulnerable you really are. Well, I decided I never wanted this to happen again to my family. I never wanted Rae-Rae to experience this kind of defenseless-ness and humiliation. But, paradoxically, this "rock bottom" really helped motivate me. I would no longer use money as an excuse. I would do everything necessary to ensure money or the lack thereof no longer controlled my fate and the safety of my family.

I hope you don't judge me for this, or assume I'm talking about materialism or greed. I'm talking about a sense of security (I mean real security, not the *illusion* of security). I'm talking about an intense desire to never be in the position again where we'd be dependent on some soulless bureaucrat at the other end of a customer service line. I'm talking about the security that comes from a constant, flowing prosperity.

We started to realize that we needed to think about money differently, that it wouldn't work for us to just keep slaving away for low wages. I wish my parents had thought differently about finances. Meaning well, they'd instilled in me pretty limited ways of thinking about money. From their experience, you couldn't expect anything more than working hard for someone else for decades, maybe saving a little bit if you were lucky, then getting a pocket watch on the last day you clocked out. Naturally, they wanted the best for me, but they didn't understand there were ways other than that usual, depressing prescription.

So we decided to go for broke, to play that big "lottery," a straight gamble, but with the deck stacked in our favor. After Raven got all that attention from strangers insisting that "she oughta be in pictures," and after her early success modeling in Georgia, we decided to go "over the top." I was done aiming for the bronze medal. So New York, here we come. We all went together as a team, and that meant we had to quit our jobs. I know that sounds counterintuitive (that's not the word my mother-in-law used!). We had a Nissan 280Z and a Mazda RX7, and we sold one. We left our apartment, good riddance. We gave ourselves no way out, because we left nothing to come back to. And we gave ourselves a year to make it all happen and dedicated ourselves wholly to the task. You know what happened.

So what can you take away from this as a parent with an individual set of personal circumstances and an equally ambitious child?

First: Know you don't need to be rich to be able to help your children's dreams come true. You just need enough to keep them—and you—safe and secure. You don't have to climb the corporate ladder, or constantly sacrifice your time with your children in favor of your job. If you choose to support your children's quest to realize their dreams, it's okay that you're not kissing behind at the office. If, on the other hand, you have any inkling of an entrepreneurial spirit, a nagging voice telling you that you ought to seize the reins and take control of your financial destiny, now's the time to act on it. The more independent you are, the more flexible you'll be to adapt (not to say it won't be hard work).

Second: If you want for your children the kind of money that we wanted, the kind of money that provides them prosperity, then you have to lead with your brain, and teach them to do the same. Teach them not to assume they have to follow the masses to go-nowhere, thankless stints in those pens they call cubicles, for forty-odd years working for the Man. That's not a life if you dream of the stars. If you always think small about money, you're always going to get small money in return. We thought big for Raven, and she made big money. It wasn't for us. We don't have that money. It's her money, that she earned, and it gives us huge satisfaction to know we helped her become a top Hollywood earner. Most important, no one will ever turn off her utilities.

Your children's dreams will probably be different: They might want to be the first person to walk on Mars, or they might want to rescue orphaned rhinos in Africa. In any case, it will be their achievement, and if you help them think big about it, they will get big results for themselves—and you'll get big gratification when you see them living it. You can read more about this in "Dream Catcher Eight: Be You."

Third: Consider the wisdom of thinking of money as a useful means to an end, not the end in itself. When the goal is the money it tends to elude you. If, on the other hand, you focus on your passion for what you're pursuing, your love of your craft, your commitment to succeeding, and your belief in your abilities, money seems to fall out of the sky on you as a reward. If you think I'm nuts for saying that, try humoring me: It really works. That's the only way our formula for Raven worked—she always loved what she was doing, and money followed the love. People often get the famous Bible quote wrong by assuming it says, "Money is the root of all evil." It does not say that. It says, "The *love of money* is the root of all evil" (1 Timothy 6:10). Big difference. Another popular misconception was epitomized by the Notorious B.I.G. in his song "Mo Money Mo Problems" (with Puff Daddy and Mase). Well, I think the theme of that song's a lot of BS. The problems you've got have nothing to do with the money. In short, money or the lack thereof should never be a justification for bad attitudes, or bad behavior. When looked at in a healthy and balanced way, money provides a nearly unlimited source of opportunity. I'll go into more detail about money in "Dream Catcher Five: Get Real."

No Education

You've probably heard the cliché stories about Thomas Edison's school sending him home because they didn't think he could learn, or Louis Pasteur's teacher rating him the worst chemistry student in his class. It just goes to show that schooling doesn't always correlate to smarts.

Too Cool for School?

Half of all the CEOs of *Fortune* 500 companies had "C" or "C-minus" averages in college.

65 percent of all U.S. senators were in the bottom half of their school classes.

75 percent of U.S. presidents were in the bottom half of their school classes.

More than half of all millionaire entrepreneurs in America never went to or finished college.

Benjamin Franklin had very little formal education.

Presidents Washington, Jackson, Van Buren, (William Henry) Harrison, Taylor, Fillmore, Lincoln, Johnson, Cleveland, and Truman never got college degrees.

Harry S Truman famously said, "The 'C' students run the world." He might have been referring to his predecessor, Franklin D. Roosevelt, a "C" student at Harvard.

I'm not saying that I don't value education, and I'm certainly not saying that you shouldn't promote a solid education for your children. In fact, I'll talk extensively about formal education in "Dream Catcher Five: Get Real." Here, I'm only suggesting you don't use your perception of your *own* educational "limitations" to give up on pursuing your children's dreams, nor assume that it necessarily follows that your children need a high-priced education in order to do well in life. You're reading a book right now by a guy who decided college (Georgia State) was not right for him—although it was "right" in a certain way, because I solidified my sense of self there. If you used a computer today, you can thank another famous dropout, Bill Gates, who ditched Harvard his junior year to get Microsoft off the ground. He was later given an honorary Harvard degree— after making billions, giving away hundreds of millions, getting knighted, and changing the world profoundly.

The bottom line is that if you really feel limited by a lack of education, go educate yourself. Find experts in the fields your children wish to pursue, and make them mentors to both of you. "A single conversation across the table with a wise man is better than ten years' mere study of books," writes Henry Wadsworth Longfellow. If it makes sense to do so, seek out experts in life-coaching, success, and motivation, and learn everything you can from them. And despite what Longfellow said above, books can also be useful, of course. When you choose those books yourself—and study them of your own free will because you want to learn—that knowledge tends to stick better than when you're forced to learn something in school.

Finally, I notice that a lot of people use learning as a pretext for *not doing*. If you ask even really gifted and dedicated professors of drama, design, fashion, and poetry whether they think their students would be better off spending less time in the hallowed halls and more time practicing their craft in the "real world," you might be surprised by what they say. A few years ago the dean of a prestigious journalism school told a group of college journalists *not* to apply to his grad school in journalism, but instead to go out and start actually doing journalism, building their experience, their "clips," and learning the trade from the inside out.

So don't stress if you're not a PhD. You know about life. You know about living. You can teach yourself, and find others to teach you everything you need to know about the field of your children's dreams.

Take Final Inventory

What else is on your list of life circumstances that might be holding you back from launching your children toward their dreams? Are you burdened by caring for your elderly parents? Are you wrapped up in tons of volunteer work? It would be inaccurate, not to mention crass, to call these things "excuses" for not dedicating yourself to your children's dreams. Of course these things are real, and they require your time and energy. All I'm saying is that you can put into your children *what* you've got, *when* you've got it. And you can usually find ways to increase the "what" and the "when" in that equation, if you make choices that support your decision to optimize yourself as a resource. I assure you that you've got everything you need to start making your children's dreams come true. What are you waiting for? Make it happen.

Do You Believe Anything Is Possible?

Perhaps more than anything, in order to optimize your children's chances of reaching their dreams, you have to believe that anything's possible. Don't spoil your children's imaginations. Don't minimize their hopes or ignore them. Don't convince your kids of the laundry list of obstacles in their way. Support your kids' determined little souls. We parents sometimes forget how our "mature" reactions to childlike dreams can affect our children's self-esteem and vision. Sure, we don't mean to hurt them when we do it, but the effect is the same. We might say, "But honey, the little boys don't want you to play baseball with them; you're a girl." Or, "That college is too expensive," or, "You can't become a singer; it's not practical."

I often wonder—and shudder to think about—what would have happened if I didn't believe in Raven's dream of getting on *The Cosby Show*. What if I had simply bought her a poster from the show?

If you're still skeptical about the power of belief, imagine uttering the words today that were so pervasive not only when I was a child, but just a few years ago: "Kid, no one will ever elect a black president." Aha! You see, anything is possible, given hard work, determination, and patience. To my mother, who grew up in Georgia on the same land where her ancestors were whipped (and who remembers all too well the back of the bus and the "colored" water fountain), the results of the 2008 election are no less than, well . . . miraculous. This just goes to show that miracles really do happen. If you believe they can.

It's really that simple. All bets are off now, folks. Second-guess your first instinct of what is possible and realistic. Even if you're trying to "protect" your child, or save them from the pain you suffered as a young dreamer, and even if their dreams seem "impossible" to you. You've got to believe in the "unbelievable."

Consider the Alternative

If your children get the message from you (and they will get the message sooner or later) that their dreams are moot, unachievable, silly, preposterous—what do you think will happen? Not only will they stop sharing their dreams with you, but they will stop dreaming. And you will be responsible for having hit the "kill switch" on their dreams. Yikes! That'd be an awful place to find yourself.

I'm not saying that you can't "keep it real" when you discuss your children's dreams. I'll talk about that later in "Dream Catcher Five: Get Real." But rest assured there's a big difference between acknowledging and expressing certain "facts on the ground" (like specific financial constraints) and *imposing* our own limitations, fears, and insecurities on our children's dreams, to crush them like bugs.

HOW TO BE LIKE MIKE'S MOTHER

Michael Jordan's mother relates how she learned never to shut down her children's dreams with negative comments or even negative beliefs, which children can sense whether you give those beliefs voice or not. She tells the story of when Michael was eight or nine: He proudly announced to her while she cooked dinner that one day he would star in the Olympics. She said, "Of course you will." And she believed it. Now Michael Jordan might be the most beloved athlete of all time. He's the very definition of achievement and self-belief.

For almost every "star," there's a story like that.

You don't have to have a child aiming for the NBA or the NFL to see this power in action. See what happens to your children and your relationship with them, if you respond to their expression of belief with, "Wow. That's a big, cool dream for a little kid. What do you think we could do to make that happen?"

You see, your child's expression to you—that she wants to sell more Girl Scout cookies than anyone else in the troop, or raise a champion pig for the state fair, or dance with the Joffrey Ballet—is a wish wrapped up in a request for your assistance. It's a call that you can *choose* to answer.

Belief Starts with You

I know you don't always feel like answering in the affirmative. You might also feel pessimistic. But when you find yourself unhopeful and beaten down, just remember all of the spectacular basketball players who happen to be short. Remember that Beethoven was all but *deaf*, and Mozart just a little kid when he started composing some of his most enduring symphonies. Remember that a ragtag band of NASA staff brought the doomed Apollo 13 crew home from space with duct tape and spare parts. You're going to have to work on yourself first to pull this off. Convince yourself. Remind yourself that anything is possible, no less in your own life than your children's. Just look around you for evidence. All the outlandish dreams of our fathers and mothers have come true. And so, too, will our children's dreams. Beyond what we can even imagine. But you've got to believe.

I never knew how much my life would change when I turned my focus on my child. And yours can, too. So start taking steps today—even little steps—in the right direction, toward helping them realize their dreams. You might have a seriously talented kid. You might have a kid with world-class dreams. You might have a kid who simply wants to accomplish some goal that might seem simple to you, but looms large in their dreams, and can't be realized without you. In any case, you've got to be up to the task. If you get your own house in order first, your kid is halfway there. You've got an awesome responsibility as a parent, but it's awfully exciting, too, and I bet that regardless of your own aspirations and accomplishments, you'll never be involved in anything as exhilarating and gratifying as standing by your children as they strive to achieve.

Dream Catcher One

Pay Attention

*The greatest gift you can give another
is the purity of your attention.*

—Richard Moss, author and inspirational speaker

The first Dream Catcher helps you "tune in" to what your children say, and what they display in terms of talents, abilities, and interests, the way I did with Raven. You'll find advice to help you guide your children to tune in to themselves, too, with the goal of increasing "reception" to what their spirit is transmitting to them. It demonstrates the important distinction between what *you* might want for your children and what your children truly want for themselves. It also lays the groundwork for the laser-like focus that will become necessary for you and your children to hone as you embark on this exciting journey.

When I Learned to Pay Attention

By 1973, my family had moved from a brief stint in Atlanta to Decatur, Georgia. My brother Andre left the house for college, and I felt like I lost my best friend. On the other hand, I gained the basement room he vacated. The room was little more than a windowless dungeon, but it was all the sanctuary I ever wanted. I was just turning thirteen, and I finally had relative privacy. I had my own color TV down there, inherited from my brother. I had long since graduated from the *Flintstones*, *Super Friends*, and *Fat Albert*, and was watching *Soul Train* now, religiously (I also loved *Bewitched*, but that's another story). My favorite show, however, was *The Tonight Show* with Johnny Carson. I watched it every night in 1974.

One of my idols was Bill Cosby, whom I'd seen on Jack Paar when I was little, as well as on his own shows, starting with *I Spy* in 1965. Cosby was the first African-American star of a TV show, and that was a huge deal (some stations down south even refused to air it). His albums in the 1960s were hilarious, and spoke to me in a way that no one had before. It wasn't that his act was about race—in fact he barely ever mentioned being black. Merely his presence on the national stage was enough to make a giant impact on me and my friends.

Cosby was a guy who, let's face it, looked a lot more like me than Johnny Carson. He was from the 'hood in Philly. His mother was a maid, and his father was a navy cook. Like mine, his dad was gone a lot in the service, so he was raised mostly by his mom. I related to him, too, because he had been a smart kid and pretty popular (class president and all)—but he failed tenth grade because he was overextended with sports, and busy acting (like I did) the class clown. It was a heady feeling watching Cosby, knowing that I could do something like that. *I'm in no way comparing myself to Bill Cosby*, by the way! I'm just saying that seeing him up there was my first real awareness of my potential. I knew I wouldn't have fit on the set of *Bewitched*, but seeing Cosby on *Carson* made me realize I could dream big, and might achieve my dreams as he had done, despite the ridiculous odds. Once, Cosby was on Carson with Mohammed Ali, and that was crazy for a kid like me to see. My parents remembered well the indignities of the Jim Crow days—segregated schools, restaurants, and so on—but now two of America's most beloved stars were black. The world was changing so fast, it gave me chills. It was a cool time to be thirteen.

Eventually, Cosby started to act as guest host on *The Tonight Show*, and I really looked forward to those nights. I remember seeing him rub Carson's desk for good luck one night, and in that moment I had a very clear vision, a kind of waking dream, that I would perform that ritual someday. I would meet both those men, and sit on those chairs. I was sure of it. I guess that's where my Hollywood dreams began.

Fast forward to 1991: Raven did *The Tonight Show*, just before Carson retired. I was waiting in the wings, and after the show I rubbed the desk just as Cosby had done. It struck me as I looked at Raven sitting beside Johnny that I had dreamt this moment, down there in my basement room, so many years before. I had let myself slowly become aware of the dream, and I didn't abort it. I didn't starve it. I didn't let it get snuffed out by naysayers and cynics—even my own parents, who tended to be more "realistic," having gone through what they went through. Instead, I nurtured that dream. I fed it and watered it. I paid attention to it, the way I'd have paid attention to anything I wanted to grow. Now Raven was the manifestation, the blooming of that dream. She was living the kind of life that, as a child, I'd imagined was possible. She was living the kind of life Lydia and I had dreamt for her. I was enormously blessed to be able to join her.

By this time, I had already spent a lot of time on *The Cosby Show* set, and once "Mr. C." and I were friends, I finally told him how much he'd meant to me as a young man. I tried not to gush (he's not the kind of guy you want to gush around) when I told him about what it was like for me to see my child on his show, interacting with him daily, helping him out, being his daughter for half an hour a week. It was, I think I remember saying, "an internal combustion," to be part of that. He laughed. And in between our constant joking behind the scenes on the show (for some reason he used to razz me about wearing "old man shoes"), Cosby shared with me that he was proud of what Raven had achieved, and what I had achieved. That's a dream come true—and my wish for you and your children.

Tune In

I recall my incredible journey from my basement to Burbank because it reminds me of the importance of hearing and heeding your calling. It all starts with *attention*. My little antennae were out when I was fifteen listening to all the far-distant signals of the Universe, and this is the station they picked up. I could have kept turning the dials but instead I tuned in, cocked my ear, and kept adjusting the controls until the signal was loud and clear. The Universe was playing my song. And when they play your song, you've got to dance.

So this is the first Dream Catcher principle: *Pay attention.* Teach your children to listen to their hearts, their souls, their little voices. Anyone can do this with some practice. You can explain that it's like a vibration or a frequency or a signal or a radio wave; whatever analogy works to get the point across. But you have to stop and listen in order to pick it up.

I can't imagine what might have happened had I not connected with Cosby as a teenager, from across those television waves. Maybe I would never have believed in myself. Maybe I would have given up hope. Maybe my on-and-off friendships with the bad boys of Decatur would have led me down a very different path. I'm certain Cosby's barrier-breaking paved the way for me and millions of others toward a limitless potential. And it makes me shiver to think it, but perhaps without my idol, I might have said to my firstborn, "No, sweetheart, you're a little black girl, so you'll never be a TV star. Why don't you consider a more down-to-earth career?" Raven wanted more. Once I understood that, I made it my sole occupation, my sole desire, to do everything in my power to help make it happen. Move a mountain? No problem. Part the seas. Done. There were no limits. I wanted to be *her* Bill Cosby. And as I sat there in the Carson studio in "beautiful downtown Burbank" with my daughter that March, I realized that millions of people were watching her now, continuing to break barriers. In our small and humble way, we were making history, and perhaps changing the lives of perfect strangers across the airwaves.

Since Raven was born, I had paid attention to the overwhelming sense of optimism and hope that flowed through me. I was attentive to her boundless potential, too. I could hear and feel and practically taste the amazing future to come. I want those same feelings for you now. For some, it might take some practice, some "tuning" of those dials. It might take going to a quiet place, a place to meditate—formally or informally—and listen to what's out there. And it might take reconnecting with your children, spending more time, asking more questions, watching more, listening more, scrutinizing, paying more attention. Through that search will come an awareness of your children's dreams and of their potential. And you'll be on the same station. You'll gain the ability to broadcast to your child on that station, to keep bolstering them with alerts about their great future, and soft, subliminal messages of encouragement.

OVERLOAD: THE COMPETITION FOR YOUR CHILDREN'S ATTENTION

Over the years, the competition has gotten greater for the attention of our children. Movies, TV, videogames, the Internet, and cell phones have captured their attention, and we parents need to gain it back. But the battle will be a tough one. Hell, our kids have DVD players in their car seats now! And have you seen what's on the media menu? With a few exceptions, like Disney, it's pretty much all violence, sex, drugs, and the proverbial rock-and-roll. I was fortunate because Raven was on *Cosby* at such a young age, and that required my supervision, so we could be together 24/7. I got to coach her, teach her, talk to her, in a kind of "total immersion." Not so for most parents. You probably have to work. You don't even see your child between 7:00 A.M. and 5:00 P.M.—or for some of you, maybe as late as 8:00 P.M. Right away, it's bedtime, and the cycle starts all over. And besides the glut of technology, what else has your children's attention? Or *who* else? Who's in your children's heads all day? It's mostly their peers and their teachers. Someone else's ideas, thoughts, and beliefs are bombarding them. You're trying to raise your child according to your morals and your values. But how do you do that when others have their attention far more than you? What advice can I give when this war seems hopelessly lost?

Well, to begin with, you can gain back a lot of their attention by getting as involved as possible in their daily lives. It seems to me that the best and strongest parents somehow have their children's attention even when they're not in the same room. You know what I mean. If your station is loud and clear enough, it can actually drown out the others, even when you think you're out of range. So during the time you are with your children, you must be focused on imparting your morals and beliefs in them.

I know you're exhausted when you get home from work. But now's not the time to slack off. You've got to pick your game up. Ask them about their homework. Ask them what they learned. "Who are your friends?" "What did you do today?" I'm not talking about giving them the third degree in an intimidating way. And I don't suggest judging or criticizing what they share. I'm just talking about getting into their heads and getting their attention back, by gaining their confidence and their trust. We do this by simply *paying attention* to them.

When we pay this kind of attention to them—especially when they're young—they cannot help but pay attention back. Children's brains are like organic computers, and we can change their software, we can reprogram them. We just have to learn their particular code, their programming language. The only way to do that is to pay very careful, close attention, as much as possible, starting as early as we can.

Attention Must Be Paid

But how exactly do you, the parent, "tune in" to what your children say, and what they display in terms of talents, abilities, and interests, the way I did with Raven? Well—pay attention! When you're with them, really be with them. Be in the moment. Imagine you're an anthropologist studying some new tribe. You have to observe. You have to interview. What are their customs? What are their beliefs? What do they think about death? The future? Themselves? The meaning of life? What are their limiting beliefs? What are they good at? What do they keep doing? What patterns emerge (athleticism, artistic skill, verbal acuity, social interaction, humor, and so forth)?

For your anthropological field report on your own children, here's a checklist of questions. You can glean answers to these questions just by some unobtrusive "spying." See if you can complete the list after two-week's study.

Get to Know Your Children by Watching Them

1. What do they reach for?
2. What do they surround themselves with?
3. What toys never see the dark of the toy chest?
4. What games get played over and over?
5. Where do they go first in a store?
6. In the mall?
7. While surfing the channels, what makes them stop and watch?
8. Where do their eyes linger when sightseeing?
9. What do they always ask questions about?
10. What subjects in school (if applicable) are they good at?
11. Who are their friends?
12. What qualities do they seem to like about their friends?
13. What do they like to wear?
14. At what activities do they seem like they're having the most fun?
15. When do they smile?
16. What makes them laugh?
17. What celebrities do they like?
18. What sports, if any?
19. What are their favorite objects besides toys?
20. What's on their night table?
21. What do they keep in their pockets?
22. What have they asked you to buy them lately?
23. What do they do when they don't think anyone's looking?
24. What places seem to fascinate them?
25. What makes them get up early?

You can imagine that once you have answers to a list like this completed, you can start to put together a picture of your children's *motivations*. You can search for patterns and for meaning in the answers. What will emerge is a profile of a certain kind of child, a child driven by certain interests and certain acumen. With this profile in place, you can start to experiment with directing your children toward the activities that fit this profile. If Sarah always looks up at planes in the sky, if she asks questions about flight, if she loved to go with you to pick up relatives at the airport, and she wears a bracelet with a hang glider on it . . . well—*pay attention*! This girl wants to fly!

Once you determine what your children are interested in, you can continuously flood them with their desires, and ultimately, their mind changes. I mean literally. Of course I'm not talking about forcibly "brainwashing" your children. Rather, I mean simply allowing them to spend more and more time with the stuff of their dreams. As they begin to focus on the attainment of their dreams, their synapses change. It's like learning a different language. New nerve connections are actually formed. This is our goal.

Get the Scoop

Now, as part of your field study, you also get to interview your subject, assuming he or she is old enough to talk. Here are some questions that you can ask directly. Do this subtly, slyly, so it doesn't feel like the Inquisition. Some questions you can ask outright, as conversation starters. And some will arise organically at other times, as responses to stuff happening around you. Some you can ask by sharing your own answer first, then asking your child what she thinks. If you can get answers to all these questions within a month or so, you get the Dream Catcher gold star award. Obviously, you should only ask the questions that are age appropriate for your children. Resist the temptation, if your children are old enough, to just give them these questions in survey form. Although some might relish it, most will probably see it as either a test or an intrusion, and they won't give spontaneous answers. Also, you'll miss the opportunity to engage with them.

Get to Know Your Children by Talking with Them

1. Do you have any recurring dreams and if so, what are they about?
2. If you won the lottery and never had to work for your whole life, what would you do with your time?
3. If you could live anywhere in the world, where would it be?
4. If you could do any job out there, what would you pick?
5. How important do you think being rich is?
6. How important do you think being happy is?
7. Who are your idols? Whom do you admire most?
8. If you had to pick one subject in school to do all day, which one would it be?
9. If you could learn about anything at all in school, what do you wish they would teach you?
10. Where would you most like to visit on our next vacation?
11. What's the coolest thing you can imagine happening to you?
12. What's your all-time favorite movie, and why?

13. What's the best advice you ever got?
14. What would make for the perfect day?
15. If you could go anywhere right now, where would it be?
16. What do you think you're really good at?
17. What would you like to get better at?
18. If you could pick one talent or skill you'd love to have—but don't have now—what would it be?
19. If school were canceled for a week, what would you do?
20. If you were going to be a teacher for a day, what would you teach?

Along these same lines, paying attention to what repels, frightens, or disgusts your children can also be valuable in assessing who they are, helping them hone their interests, and getting them closer to their dream state. Children who faint at the sight of blood will need either to stay away from veterinary school, or somehow get over their problem. Either way, it's good to have a sense of this potential challenge up front.

Mad Skills

It's worth noting here that you don't have to be an expert in social psychology to notice there's usually an innate correlation between acumen (talent, skill, ability) and interest. A child who plays some rugby and begins to get better will usually keep playing, and therefore get better, and therefore keep playing (because the rewards are great: internally, a feeling of accomplishment, self-possession, mastery—and externally, attention, popularity, trophies). This makes the process easier for the parent, because all you have to do is follow your children's lead. You encourage their interest, you help increase their acumen, you provide more opportunities to pursue the interest, and you keep on rewarding them. They probably got into rugby in the first place—instead of, say, boat-building—because of a synthesis of personality quirk and predisposition (genetic, cultural, or God-given). You might have even introduced them to the interest, nudging them in a certain direction because you sensed or noted the kernels of the acumen: *Even as a baby, Jane had great coordination and grace, so we knew she'd make a great dancer. As expected, when we enrolled her in her first ballet class, she blossomed. . . .* Or, *Jack started speaking at one, and putting words together so poetically at five that we just assumed he'd make a wonderful writer. We had a feeling if we introduced him to some great poetry, he'd really take off, and sure enough. . . .* See, it all kind of just makes sense. Interests suit acumen, and your role as parent is to facilitate the natural process. People say about a child, "He's a natural," and this is what they mean. When you add a supportive environment to motivation and acumen, you help your child develop mastery in his or her chosen discipline.

A Fad, or a Dream?

Sometimes it's not immediately clear to you that your child's current interest reflects a real commitment, or is the first step in a big dream. It might just be a phase or temporary interest. If you're wondering how you determine whether they're revealing just a whim and not a bona fide dream worth pursuing, the answer is often easy: Passing fancies, by definition, pass. Those wishes that take hold and endure will reveal themselves and be totally transparent. And their intensity will be clear. Don't worry—you usually can't miss them.

But every once in a while, it might be hard to tell. Say Sam expressed an interest in the math club in seventh grade. He stuck it out, seemed to like it, and now that he's in eighth, he can join the Mathletes, the school's competitive math team, which travels the state competing in league competition. Sam doesn't make it obvious that he's a "math geek" like some of the other kids do. And he's got other stuff going on his life, including CPR classes and building model ships. So how do you assess his seriousness about the math club? You don't want to push. **You don't want to give Sam the feeling, by your enthusiasm, that he *should* continue, or else disappoint you. It's not about you.** Here are some questions you can ask to determine your children's level of commitment, and thus plan for your level of support. Some of these questions are adapted from Marsha Delcourt's "What Parents Need to Know about . . . Recognizing Interests, Strengths, and Talents of Gifted Adolescents," a practitioner's guide from the National Research Center on the Gifted and Talented. Remember to tailor the question based on age-appropriateness:

Whim or Dream?
- Is this something you're doing mainly for hanging out with the other kids?
- Is this something you're doing because you actually like the competition?

- Is this something that gives you a big sense of accomplishment?
- Is this something you really want to get better at?
- Is this something you can see yourself doing for the long term?

Mom, Dad, I'm Really Serious

If it becomes clear through such questioning and a careful review of your children's practice that they are indeed serious about pursuing this dream, you now have another set of questions to ask.

You and your son or daughter have to begin to focus on developing their talents for the long term, in order to move them toward achieving their dream.

Is it *really* fun? Do you get real enjoyment out of it? If not, it will be hard to keep up your motivation. What about it is fun? Is it intellectually stimulating? Physically challenging? Socially rewarding?

Do you need outside validation to make you "successful" at it? Is it something like martial arts or boxing where there are contests, competitions, tournaments, and so on, in which you need to participate? There are obvious upsides and downsides to this. Is it something like play writing that you can pursue individually, but might eventually need the support of others to "put on the show"? Or is it something you can pursue entirely on your own, like hiking?

What's it going to cost? Are there associated costs for memberships, equipment, training, etc.? Are the costs reasonable? If they're exorbitant (it's pretty expensive to transport horses around the country for rodeo riding, for example), then what's the plan for financing the dream? Is there some kind of monetary limit over which the family can't go?

Will you need a special trainer, tutor, or coach? If so, is this someone you can find locally? How will you finance special instruction if necessary?

Will you have to travel extensively to pursue the dream? If so, can you afford it? Are there scholarships available, or not-for-profit foundation grants that can help defray the costs? Can the family find the time and other resources necessary to support these road trips?

Will the skills developed to pursue this dream help in other aspects of life? Will you learn valuable competencies that are universal or transferable—leadership skills, poise, balance, physical prowess, higher-order thinking, visual acuity, etc.?

Are there true long-term prospects for the pursuit of this dream? Can you count on an indefinite run?

Can you find a way to balance this dream with your other responsibilities? Will a vigorous quest for this dream conflict with school, for example? Is there a way to make reasonable adjustments?

Can this dream lead to a lucrative or at least comfortable career? Can you eventually make money pursuing your dream, so that you won't have a potential conflict between "work" and the dream?

As you uncover answers to these questions, keep "adjusting the dial" of your attention.

Keeping the "Troops" in Line

With all this talk about putting your children's dreams front and center, you might think I'm advising you to put your *children in charge* of your household. Let me be perfectly clear: *no way.* I took my advice from my good friend—and my son Blaize's godfather—Dr. Vito Guarnaccia, a psychologist, and his wife, Elizabeth, a clinical social worker. Together they wrote a parenting guide called *Rules of Engagement,* in which they remind parents that parenting is tantamount to a military operation. Each parent needs to think of himself or herself as the commanding officer, on duty at all times. The mission is to get the children through the battlefield of their youth and over to the other side—adulthood—as unscathed as possible. During this operation, the lives of the "troops" are literally in the hands of the parent-generals.

This is not say you should run your house like an army. It simply means that healthy children grow up with a healthy fear and respect for authority—and you and your spouse are the main authority figures. A healthy fear means that children are concerned about the consequences for inappropriate behavior. Of course, consequences for unacceptable behavior should **never** be emotionally or physically harmful, but they should be *meaningful* if they're going to work as disincentives. Children should want to please their parents, and not disappoint them. This doesn't mean that you should teach your children to blindly obey you, or to not think critically about their decisions (they're not supposed to actually salute you!). It simply means that while your family dynamic allows for occasional disagreements, you have the ultimate say about all critical decisions—and your decisions are binding. It's not a democracy.

When parents establish this clear chain-of-command early on, they create stability, security, predictability, and a healthy sense of respect for authority. All of these are critical ingredients to create an environment that nurtures dreams and paves the way to healthy, productive, and successful adulthood.

~

The Parent Station, 24/7

Finally, I want to remind you that as you train your children to tune in to themselves, you should broadcast your own station, all day long, with a signal so clear they can hear it even when they're away at summer camp, or behind their school messing around with friends. Tune them in, and keep tuning them in. Your station will be upbeat, motivational, inspirational, and fun, but with the same, constant underlying message.

On the Christopher B. Pearman Station, I broadcast to baby Rae-Rae day and night. The message streaming was, "You're the greatest. You can do anything!" When I picture myself leaning over her crib like that, whispering constant positivity, I see I really was like a Dream Catcher, filtering out the bad, and propagating only the good down into my baby's consciousness. Your Parent Station, too, should be like a Dream Catcher antenna whose signal is so strong it wipes out all the negative messages the world sends your children on its million other stations. In fact, as broadcast manager, you can filter all the other stations, or at least translate those you can't quiet, to ensure *your message*—the message that your children can achieve anything—still gets through the loudest and clearest.

This deep and abiding faith in your children, and a willingness to *communicate* that faith to them on a station loud and clear and constantly in tune, is where this awesome journey begins for you and your children.

Dream Catcher Two

Believe It

Man is made by his belief. As he believes, so he is.

—*Bhagavad-Gita*, ancient Hindu text

The second Dream Catcher shows you how to stack the deck in favor of your child's achievement by *believing that anything is possible*. You will communicate to them through your words, actions, and feelings either your optimism or your pessimism, both of which will influence their own beliefs. We'll explore the self-belief that was at the core of Raven's and my success together. **Anything is possible, given hard work, determination, and patience—but it all starts with belief.**

Finding the Inner Belief

When I was a teenager, I was pretty mature for my age. By this, I mean I did a lot of mature thinking—even as I engaged in a few juvenile antics. I'd always thought as deeply as I could about "what it all means." As a young child, I had stared up at the moon in the woods behind our house in Connecticut, and wondered where I fit into the big picture. I felt certain I could touch the moon, somehow, if only I could *wish* it strongly enough. And when I got older, as happens, I looked more inwardly, at a light even stronger than the reflection from the moon. Thinking about this period in my life reminds me of a quote by Ralph Waldo Emerson: "Belief consists in accepting the affirmations of the soul; unbelief, in denying them." Sometimes, I thought so long and hard about the meaning of life, and dreamed so big about all my potential, that it almost hurt. You understand what I mean. Philosophers call those kinds of thoughts "existential quandaries"—you know, "I think, therefore I am."

The "Chosen People"

I had a momentous experience one day when I was around seventeen. I had grown up in the church—sometimes Presbyterian, sometimes Baptist, the usual denominations down south, where we'd moved when I was about eleven. But there were some Jews in our neighborhood, too, and some were friends. One day, one of my Jewish friends said to me, very matter-of-factly, that he was among the "Chosen People." I looked at him a moment as though he was some kind of alien, but he didn't back down. Right away I felt deeply, like in the marrow of my bones, a kind of desperate "uh-oh." The implication of my friend's announcement, at least in my interpretation, was that *I* was *not* a "chosen" person. You can imagine how profoundly disturbing this revelation was to me. When I found my mother in the kitchen later, I told her what had happened, and asked her, "What about me? Why am I not a chosen person?"

Needless to say, she was not pleased with that boy's comment (my mother was one of sixteen children if you can believe it, so I suppose she was used to not being a "chosen one"). She tried to make me feel better. She told me what she thought the boy had meant, and she told me it wasn't true, despite how some people construe the Bible, that some were chosen by God, and others somehow forsaken. But none of it sunk in. And so, for a very unsettling time, I believed that kid. I felt left out. I mean in a *big* way, left out, like left out of the plan of the Universe. And then, staring up at the ceiling in my basement room one night while listening to my beloved Earth Wind & Fire, I got a kind of message from the world I'd believed had given up on me. It said, *I choose you. I choose everyone.* It was not the voice of some Old Man God on a heavenly throne, like Charlton Heston hears from the pillar of fire in *The Ten Commandments*, but rather like the Source of all things talking to me, on some kind of cellular level. And I was all at once overcome with the knowledge that it was true: We are all "chosen" people. Of course we are! We're all one. It doesn't make sense that some wonderful and mysterious force created the Universe, then decided "I like this guy better than that guy." That would be absurd. It would be like saying that my parents loved me more than my brother, or vice versa, or I loved one of my children more than the other.

So I started to read. Down in my sacred dungeon of a room with the soundtrack to *Saturday Night Fever* playing over and over. I found a little bit of truth in everything, and found that some of it was now disjointed and conflicting, but some of it had common denominators. One is that *we have the power*. We are chosen. And even though some have come who have walked on water because their belief was so strong, that's not supposed to stop us from being gods in our own life, from performing little miracles every day in how we live our lives.

YOU ARE CHOSEN

All children invariably feel insecure at times, as though they're all alone in a cold world. Remind them that we're all "chosen people." You can say, "We chose to have you (or adopt you, or foster you) and we chose to take care of you, keep you safe, and try to make you happy. And in the same way, we are all chosen, deliberately, for some special purpose. Let's find that purpose together. And at the core of being a "chosen person" is to *choose to believe in yourself.*

That kid did me a huge favor that day. He started a chain of consequences in my mind and soul that made me who I am today. But what's the point of including that in this book? It's an important story to convey for five big reasons:

First, to get across to you that you can help your children recover and thrive after painful experiences, by talking to them about your own struggles in youth, your own pain. It's likely that whatever their age, your children see you as insurmountably older, practically from another time and dimension. And this is partially true. But I know that when I told my son and daughter of my epiphany and the painful events that led up to it, they saw me, even for a flickering moment, as someone they could relate to, someone who, on some level, was a friend (a friend dressed in 1970s outfits maybe, but a friend nonetheless!).

Second, I include this story because it reminds me that children often see their parents as Godlike and infallible. I think it's critical to be a strong, confident, knowledgeable parent, the way my mother and father were, and the way my wife and I tried to be. But there is a lot of room there for expressing insecurity, too, or maybe you could call it "agnosticism." **You don't know everything. You don't *have* to know everything. You can't know *everything*.** Consider whether your children might actually gain some confidence about their thought processes if you show them by example how yours work, and how, inevitably, there are periods of uncomfortable uncertainty. The message is: *This sucks right now. But it will get better. There's sunshine behind every cloud.*

Third, this story reminds me of the power of perception. It's an object lesson in how the way you think about something creates your reality. Someone says you're not a chosen person, and it rocks your world because you believe it. You internalize it. It becomes your reality. Or someone says you're dumb. Or too fat, or whatever. I encourage you to help your child understand that merely thinking something makes it so, as Shakespeare writes. You can change your perception, and "reality" changes, too. It takes some practice, and you're never really "done" learning how to do it. But this idea and the skills that underlie it just might be the most important gift you ever give your child.

Fourth, this story illustrates that despite our many ostensible differences—color, creed, national origin, gender, and sexuality—we're all actually one. We all struggle with where we fit in. We all want to feel good. We all want to feel special, to be "chosen."

Lastly, I understand now forty-plus years later, it's a story about judging others, about hierarchy. When I look back on this experience as an adult, of course I harbor no ill feelings toward my friend who said he was chosen and I was not: He was only acting out a script that he'd inherited from his parents, and interpreting it for his own sense of security. At the time, it struck a huge nerve, of course, but he did not intend to hurt me. What I think about now is how important it was for him to believe that. There's more along these lines in "Dream Catcher Seven: Do Good." Haven't you ever noticed how important a part our relative positions in the world play in our daily lives? At the extreme, someone's always the master and someone's always the slave. But it can be more subtle than that: Some celebrities are "hot" and some are "has-beens." Some kids are "good" and some "bad." You might be a model, but you're not a "supermodel." And, interestingly, if we find ourselves on one of the bottom rungs of a given pecking order, we start to break up our category into its own hierarchy, so we can at least be closer to the top of something. Among African Americans there's a history of judgments back and forth based on the relative "lightness" or "darkness" of skin color. What's that all about? We have a deep need to one-up each other, a kind of human equivalent of that bumper sticker that says, "I may be slow, but I'm ahead of you!" It's hard to break out of this pattern, but it's possible. And it can be taught. Let your children see you competing against yourself and not others for your "personal best." Let your children see you choose the car and the road and the destination that's right for you. Then roll down your windows, put on your favorite music, lean back, tap your hand on the door, and go the speed you want to go. **It's your journey. It doesn't matter where everyone else is going, or how and when they get there. Just enjoy the ride.**

The Belief Posse

It almost goes without saying that if you want to achieve something great, you need to surround yourself with a crew of people who believe in you absolutely. You need the support and encouragement of others to get things—especially great things—done.

Edmund Hillary never would have reached the summit of Mt. Everest in 1953 without the help of Tenzing Norgay, his Sherpa and right-hand man (in fact there were more than *400 people* on the team, all focused on getting that one, big, dangerous job done safely). At one point, Sherpa Tenzing actually saved Hillary's life, quite dramatically, by jamming his ice axe into the snow and quickly lashing a rope around it, locking up Hillary before he smashed into smithereens on a block of ice at the bottom of a crevasse. For decades, neither man would say which of them had actually set foot first on the elusive summit. Instead, they always said, "It was a team effort."

For the vast majority of singular achievements that appear to be "individual," there is, in fact, a major "team effort" that accounts for the success. For each of our Olympic athletes, for example, there might be hundreds of others—coaches, assistants, trainers, agents, and so on—standing behind, both literally and figuratively, promoting, advancing, and egging them on.

It doesn't matter whether your goal is humanitarian or nefarious—even bad guys need a team of henchmen to help them achieve their evil ends. You must have people around you, constantly reminding you what you intend to do, and telling you, "You can do it. I believe in you."

At the least, your closest confidants, those around you with the most influence, must be on your side. They must believe in you unquestionably. We must help our children with big dreams understand that the attitudes and beliefs of those around us rub off on us like wet paint—and you don't want to be painted grey. So here's a five-pronged plan for building a Belief Posse to stand by your child on his or her way to the stars:

1. Impart in your child an unshakable sense of well-being, a powerful feeling that all is right with the world, and there's nothing that he or she can't achieve. Start this process early, preferably in the womb or the cradle. This force field of self-belief is critical for later deflecting the inevitable negative influences and messages that the world will try to hurl their way.

2. Make sure that you, as parent, are the most positive, constructive, encouraging role model you can be. You are the most influential person in your children's lives. So live your own life to your utmost potential, show your child through example the power of belief and all it can achieve in reality.

3. Know and "interview" all the other influential people in your child's life, such as teachers, coaches, and camp counselors. You don't have to give them the third degree. It will become obvious from a short conversation whether they're the type of people who will buoy up your children when the waves of the world come their way—or whether they will drag them down.

4. Help your children understand that their friends—the people with whom they spend the most time, and often invest the most trust—can make or break them. This is a sensitive area, because of course you want your children to pick their own friends. But if a friend was a violent drug dealer, surely your protective instinct would kick in, and you would find appropriate ways to intervene to

end that friendship. So why wouldn't you want to have a say in other kinds of negative friendships? Hopeless, angry, pessimistic friends will make it very difficult for your children to believe in anything, no less in themselves and their potential for greatness.

5. Demonstrate for your children the joy in always acting as a positive influence in other people's lives. Show them how they can always find ways to bolster their siblings and their friends, to reinforce their goals and dreams with positive thinking. Modeling belief in others will vastly enhance their self-belief, and strengthen their "friend filter," so that when choosing their own friends, they'll tend toward those who will influence them positively.

What's *Your* Problem?

If you've never seen the motivational speaker David Ring, I highly recommend him. Ring starts his talks (hundreds of times a year) by challenging the audience: "I have cerebral palsy," he says with a strong speech impediment. "What's *your* problem?" That's a wake-up call, isn't it?

I didn't exactly come from the Ivy Leagues of life. I grew up in a middle-class neighborhood, but all around me in Decatur were drug dealers and troublemakers. When I looked in the mirror I saw an African-American boy. My parents worked their asses off and had some things to show for it—a nice house and nice cars—but not the vast wealth and bounty promised by the "American Dream." The world of optimism and success were miles and miles away. But, as Ring always says, "God uses broken vessels." All we have to do is find a little bit of glue from somewhere, to keep the pieces together. I pray your children will find an idol, a mentor, a guide, a hero, even a far-distant one, as I did, to keep their pieces together. Abraham Lincoln? Barack Obama? Helen Keller? Derek Jeter? Sonia Sotomayor? Or perhaps it can be you.

Act "As If"

What if you don't believe in yourself? From where do you mine belief when the well is dry? While most people might assume that behavior follows belief (you believe in yourself, so you perform well), in fact, it works the other way around. The right, positive behaviors and actions can spur belief.

As a good example of this, consider the mighty Harvard Crimson. Some people think women's basketball is for the timid—or just the stuff of offensive punch lines by Don Imus. But these naysayers obviously didn't witness the landmark March 14, 1998, NCAA women's basketball tournament, where No. 16–ranked Harvard crushed No. 1 Stanford in one of the best upsets ever.

The Crimson-vs.-Cardinal matchup was set to be just another humiliation for the Brain Trust women of Harvard. But Harvard pulled something special from the deep well of their ambition, and treated us to the performance of a lifetime. The all-American Allison Feaster scored 35 points, which catapulted Harvard into a one-point lead with a little more than a minute to play. They locked it up with a clean three-pointer, and the Stanford women fell into a collective catatonic state. Until then, no Ivy League women's team had ever won a game in NCAA tournament play.

A 6-foot-4 college sophomore center from North Carolina, Melissa Johnson, watched that game in awe. She transferred to play for Harvard the next year, sidled up to the coach, Kathy Delaney-Smith, and asked her the secret to that miracle win. She described the experience—and the lessons she learned from her coach—in a March 2009 *New York Times* essay called "First Step in Becoming a Winner: Act Like One."

Any decent athlete, salesman, or Starbucks barista can put on a good "game face." But Delaney-Smith's philosophy, "Act As If," goes much deeper than mere swagger or theatrics, according to Johnson. It's a method—a learned skill—for convincing your mind that you already are what you want to become. **The body follows where the mind leads.**

"Act as if you're a great shooter," she instructed her players. "Act as if you love the drill. Act as if when you hit the deck it doesn't hurt." She did not tolerate negativity on the court, in the locker room, or during training. Even negative body language was a no-no.

So how did Harvard beat the giants of Stanford? Johnson says, in short, what the overly analytical Harvard players might have lacked in comparative speed or vertical jumping ability against Stanford, they made up with their *power of belief.*

Delaney-Smith is an awesome coach. But she didn't invent the concept of "Act As If." "If you want a quality, act as if you already had it," advised William James, the American psychologist and philosopher (himself a Harvard man).

Perhaps no figure in the recent past has exemplified James's tactic more than Barack Obama. Remember all those pundits who bemoaned Barack Obama's confident style as he toured America, Europe, and the Middle East in the run-up to the 2008 election? They actually said, "Why is he already acting like he's the president?" Well, isn't it obvious? It was as though Obama was preparing himself for a role, beginning to *embody* the presidency. And of course this technique worked. He acted as if he were the president. And now he is.

A great purveyor of transformational wisdom, Dr. Wayne W. Dyer, solidified this concept for me in his self-help book, *The Power of Intention*:

> Initiate actions that support your feelings of abundance and success. Here, the key word is actions. I've been calling this acting as if or thinking from the end and acting that way. Put your body into a gear that pushes you toward abundance and feeling successful. Act on those passionate emotions as if the abundance and success you seek is already here. Speak to strangers with passion in your voice. Answer the telephone in an inspired way. Do a job interview from the place of confidence and joy. Read the books that mysteriously show up, and pay close attention to conversations that seem to indicate you're being called to something new.

~

Teaching Children "Act As If" Techniques

You can help your children understand the Act As If notion in a couple of useful ways. To "Act As If" is not exactly like pretending, but close. In the beginning, you might have to pretend. But very soon, you're playing the part and you become the part. There's a fine line between pretending and being. And "being" something is usually just a reflection of your *believing* that you are something. So start with the belief, act accordingly, and you'll be it for real. In the meantime, when you Act As If, you get all kinds of experience necessary to hone your skills and get better at what you want to be.

For example, if you Act As If you're a champion horse jumper, you'll be gaining the experience, the persistence, and the practice you'll need to actually *be* a champion horse jumper. Meanwhile, while you Act As If you are a champion, you'll be more likely to look and feel like a champion. And with all that practice, pretty soon you'll have lots of knowledge, confidence, and even more skill.

Use your imagination when you Act As If. "Imagination is the true magic carpet," writes Norman Vincent Peale. So imagine yourself as confident while you're performing your thing. Imagine you are great at it, and everybody knows you are. A huge part of success while performing any task is confidence. Sure, you have to build your talent and skill as well, but better to build them while imagining you're confident, not stressed and insecure.

The Almost *Unbelievable* Power of Belief

In Japan, a man had a stomach tumor. They brought in healers: They surrounded this man, and prayed and chanted intensely, all "believing" the man's cells were healthy. It actually worked, and they got the evidence on film. And among people with dissociative disorder ("split personalities"), scientists have witnessed something even more incredible: The mind believes so strongly in the reality of the split personality, that the physical body actually manifests that reality—in the *same person*, one "personality" might have high blood sugar, and the other, not. One personality might even have blue eyes, and the other brown! Now *that's* the power of belief.

These anecdotes support the radical notion that there is an actual "biology of belief" (see Bruce H. Lipton's 2008 book of the same name). In short, belief is a state of mind, but it has a correlating biology behind it, perhaps even a cellular one. This means belief has real energy. And where there's energy, there's power to tap. Physicists have long noted that when one observes an electron, the mere act of observation affects the state of the electron. Well, if a mere gaze can change a single electron, what does that imply for our bodies, our minds, our Universe and how we perceive it, considering we're all made up of electrons?

But there's no need to get into quantum physics, because everyone's heard the well-documented stories of children stuck under cars until their moms single-handedly lifted up the car. Mom doesn't "think" first, doesn't "consider" whether she *can* lift the car. She just knows she has to, and believes, if just for a second, that she can, so her belief alone produces superhuman strength. In fact, the determination and belief cause surges in hormones and actually changes our physiological state drastically, so we're up to the "impossible" task. The question is, *How can we use that same power in our lives now?* I say, if the power of belief can allow a 95-pound woman to lift a 2,000-pound car, why can't it help a child become a great ice skater? Well, I think it can. The belief has to be so strong as to become part of our physical state, part of our reality. We have to "psych ourselves up" to the point where anything is possible.

It works the other way around, too. Some people say, "Oh, no. It's November. I'm going to get a cold. I get a cold every year around this time." And lo and behold, they do. These people might think they're merely predicting the inevitable, but their belief is actually telling themselves, telling their mind and body to make it happen. Belief creates the state.

Couple Belief with Action Steps

There might be such a thing in the world called "luck," and it might play a small part in some people's success. But do you want to teach your children to wait around, simply hoping for luck? That doesn't seem like a sensible prescription for success. Instead, you have to instill in them the power of belief.

But believing alone is not enough. You can *believe* you're on a hit TV show, but they'll put you away eventually if you're not moving in that direction, instead, sitting in a diner proclaiming that you're a big star. You have to put action into place along with belief. *You have to step toward your goal, or you'll always be standing still.* Raven believed she could "do what Rudy does" on *The Cosby Show*, and we believed her. So we pulled up stakes and moved to New York from Atlanta, to make the belief reality. With a firm belief and action steps toward your goal, you have all the elements necessary to achieve your goal. It will come, guaranteed. That's a law.

You're not likely to believe you will become a world-class chef, and take specific steps toward that dream with true faith and no doubt or hesitation, and "accidentally" wind up a zookeeper.

In his book *The Four Agreements*, Miguel Ruiz says we see what we "agree" to see. What we think of as reality is merely what we agree is true. What does that say? So hang this Dream Catcher over your children's heads, and let it filter out the unbelievers' doubt: *Believe it, then follow that belief—and it shall be.*

Dream Catcher Three

Picture It

We are what we think. All that we are arises with our thoughts. With our thoughts we make the world.

—Buddha

L et's now look at the breathtaking power of visualization. For millennia, athletes, artists, and leaders have used visualization to achieve spectacular ends, and you'll find some inspiring examples here. Most people don't know that the mind can't tell the difference between what you *imagine* yourself doing and what you *actually* do. You'll learn here how to visualize the kind of future you want for your children, and how to help them visualize their own success. I'll show you some of the exciting, bonding, positive-visualization exercises I employed with Raven and her brother Blaize through the years, and introduce you to other successful kids who've done the same. Finally, we'll see that *negative* visualization is formidable, too.

Start Right Away with Positive Visualization!

This might be the simplest yet most effective use of positive visualization I've found. You can practice it for a short while with very little effort until it becomes habit, then easily teach your children how to employ it in their own lives. End your day and begin your day in a quiet place, such as in bed, with a brief visualization of the day to come, with everything working out just the way you'd like. I don't mean picture wads of cash falling from the sky. Just simply see yourself in your daily environment as happy, productive, and peaceful, just going about your day with a smile and a sense of accomplishment. That's it. But I mean really *see* yourself. You'll be amazed how far this exercise can go in alleviating all that unnecessary stress about what *might* happen later today, all the things that *could* go wrong.

If you combine this practice with positive verbal reinforcement, too, it can be even more effective.

Put positive self-talk in the present tense, keep it brief, and upbeat. My favorite is, "*I am healthy, wealthy, and wise.*" Repeat to yourself or out loud, over and over, in the shower, driving to work, walking the dog, until it becomes a mantra.

If You Don't Have a Vision, What Is a Dream?

Without a clear mental picture, our dreams are fuzzy, like an unfocused photograph. Shrouded in darkness, they will eventually disappear. In order to turn our goals and dreams into reality, we have to bring that hazy picture into sharp and lifelike focus. We first have to *visualize* what our success will look like. As you help your children assess who they are, start working on *what they want*, too—help them paint a picture of it, or direct a movie in their head of what it will look like when they finally get there. If they are looking to break a world record in hang gliding, for example, remind them that they should continuously *picture* themselves hang gliding. They should paint clear and absorbing images in their head—*moving* pictures if possible—of them launching, soaring, catching updrafts, dipping, diving, and landing safely. Remind them to repeatedly picture themselves accepting their recognition from their heroes, famous and accomplished pilots and the top gliders from around the world. They should visualize themselves *being* and *feeling* like the best hang glider on the planet. Remind them to make these pictures vivid, bright, and detailed—what are they wearing? What's the weather like? What is the scenery? Remind them that the more *senses* they include in their vision—What will it feel like? Sound like? Smell like?—the stronger that vision will settle in their mind, and the more likely it will be that they *will* break that record; they will be the best hang glide ever. You see, *reality follows the vision*—it's as simple as that. What some people criticize as mere "fantasy" is actually a mental dress rehearsal for success.

The message to your children should be: Don't find yourself—*create* yourself. *Make* yourself. Invent yourself as the exact kind of *you* that you want to be. And start by visualizing this person, this you, living the kind of life you want to live, being the kind of being you want to be.

This is not my idea. Athletes discovered thousands of years ago the power of positive visualization. They discovered that to perfect a discus throw, they needed not only to practice again and again, not only to learn and hone by trial and error, not only to study others making perfect throws and attempt to emulate them, but also to *mentally replay the moves* one step at a time, over and over again. As the mind pictures the scene and plays each frame, the brain goes through its motions the same way it does when the body is actually performing the moves physically. The synapses fire, the brain chemistry percolates, and nerve pathways are formed and solidified. As a matter of fact, some interesting recent science shows that even muscles respond to this kind of mental "exercise."

The discus throw is just the beginning, of course. I will go so far as to propose that you should teach your children to visualize what their whole life will look like once they have put their dreams in motion. What will it feel like to get "A's" in social studies? What would it look like to stand up in front of my classmates as the seventh grade class treasurer? What would the crowd sound like when I blocked that shot, and won the game for my team? Today's mental pictures, if nourished and nurtured, will grow into tomorrow's authenticity.

Come Out of the Cave

Now there's a lot of practical advice in this book, but some of it has some deeper roots. So I want to introduce an idea that took me a long time to fully comprehend, but once I did, it was much easier for me to visualize my dreams for Raven, my family, and myself. I have to go way back in time to explain the concept, and look to Plato for some guidance. In his "Allegory of the Cave," we see prisoners chained, unable to move their heads, facing a wall. Behind and above them burns a fire, and between the fire and the prisoners, marionette players put on a kind of puppet show. Because the prisoners' heads are chained and their eyes are locked on what's in front of them, they see only the shadows of the objects projected onto the wall. But they have no way of knowing that what they see is not "real," but just a shadow of reality, a reflection of the "real thing." So they form all their ideas about the way things "are" from these images. Plato's point is that during our lives, we are like those prisoners, limited by the chains that bind us (the poet William Blake called them "mind-forged manacles"), and passively awaiting some projection before us, over which we have no control, and which we accept as ultimate truth. There it is, right in front of us, visible to the naked eye, so it must be true, it must be real. Thing is, though, it's just a puppet show. It just seems real. It looks real. We get caught up in it, and we suspend our disbelief, the way we do at the movies. In fact, moviemakers are so aware of "The Allegory of the Cave" that it spawned a whole franchise. I'm sure you've heard of it—it's called *The Matrix*. Think about it.

It looks real, but it isn't real. It isn't true. "Real" and "true" are what you make for yourself.

Philosophers had contemplated this paradox before, but Plato really made it clear through his allegory: The cave is a kind of self-inflicted darkness that prevents us from seeing the true objects that are behind us—and even those aren't "real," but just cutouts the puppeteers hold in front of the fire! In Plato's allegory, even the fire isn't quite "real," but just a small *model* of the sun outside that we cannot see for our chains in the darkness. In fact it's so dark in this cave, and our blinders so strong, that we can't even see each other. We can't even see our *selves*. It's deep stuff, for sure, but integral to the idea of shifting your vision.

INTRODUCING YOUR CHILDREN TO PLATO'S CAVE

You might be thinking, my children can't deal with Plato! They barely understand *The Simpsons*! But they *can* understand this. The simple lesson is: Our senses (what our mind tells us is "real") are flawed reporters of fact. In fact, there are no facts. You can't really "know" or "understand" the world around you unless you use your senses to do so, but your senses are limited, biased, easily fooled. In short, they're unreliable. The good news here is that *you* can create your own "reality." You can become the puppeteer. Ask your children, "Is that chair over there real?" When they say, "Sure," ask them, "How do you know?" They're going to say, "Because I see it." Now ask them, "Can you see arctic seabirds right now? See any penguins?" When they say, "No," you'll counter, "But aren't those real?" You can see where this is going. The ultimate goal is to get them to understand the unreliability of the senses in their construction of reality. And to get them to grasp that if they allow it—if they don't shuffle off those chains—they'll be letting *someone else*, some mysterious power behind them, run *their* puppet show.

Be the Master of Puppets

My favorite part of the cave allegory is the idea of the puppet show, the grand illusion in front of us that we assume is real. I like it because it reminds me that our children are in some way like those prisoners chained to the wall. And guess who gets to put on the "reality" show in front of them? We do. The parents. See, we get to take advantage of this situation. We get to "show" our children, every day, the way the world "really" is. We get to parade in front of the fire so that our children see in front of them the reflection of our actions and ideas. Very soon they become accustomed to believing this movie we project in front of them. So when they're young, we have to take pains to make sure the reflections are positive, and the images are magnificent.

Then as soon as they are able, we have to teach them how to break those chains, and how to hold up their own figures, their own pictures, their own ideas, their own "models," so that they unfold in front of them in living color, so that their innermost dreams are at one with what they consider their reality.

Now what does this have to do with creative and positive visualization? Well, they are one and the same thing. Remember—there is no "real." "Real" is merely what we "see" on that wall in front of us. If we are the ones doing the projecting, then "real" could be our summiting Kilimanjaro, winning a soap box derby, or learning five different languages. All we have to do is run that film, hold those silhouettes in front of the fire, and *voilà!* There they are. They become part of our consciousness. Our actions, our "reality" moves boldly toward them. There isn't a single celebrity or successful athlete who didn't first *see* him- or herself succeeding.

Putting Visualization to Work

Picturing our dream state (our success and achievements) allows us to engage with those dreams every day, and this practice actually drives us toward fulfillment. When you clearly picture the results, you're halfway to achieving them. A regimen of visualization and a practice that starts to normalize these images actually makes them real, eventually. And when we work this magic, we access a secret part of our brain that is so often ignored, to our peril. Many studies actually prove that the mind can't tell the difference between what you *imagine* yourself doing and what you *actually do*. For example, PET scans of the brain indicate that just *visualizing* the moves you'd make during a particular high dive, triggers the nerves and muscles the same way the real dive does. As a diver in high school, I used to picture my dives, over and over—the perfect execution—starting weeks before a meet, and even as I climbed the ladder to the board.

You can introduce your children to this concept early, by sharing with them the following example.

As they got ready for the all-important 1980 Olympic Games, a group of Russian coaches and scientists put together four groups of world-class athletes in order to examine the effectiveness of physical training versus mental training. The first group focused completely on physical training, with no mental training whatsoever (100 percent physical training). The second group did 75 percent physical training and 25 percent mental training. The third group did half and half. Finally, the fourth group did 25 percent physical training and 75 percent mental training. Guess what? It wasn't the first group that saw the biggest improvements in performance. This shocked people. You might think that athletes who trained the most *physically* in their sport would perform the best in completion. It wasn't even the third group, the one that split the physical and mental training evenly. It was actually the *fourth* group that improved the most, followed by group three, followed by group two and finally, group one. That's right—the group that did the *least* physical training, but the *most* mental training, became the best. That's very cool. Of course you'll notice that the top group did do *some* physical training: It would be hard to bench press hundreds of pounds if you didn't train for it physically. But more important, according to this study, you have to train for it *in your brain*. This explains why performance coaches and sports psychologists have long waiting lists and lovely homes. You can read more about the Russian Olympians and other cases in Robert Scaglione and William Cummins's book *Karate of Okinawa: Building Warrior Spirit*.

Let's look into this process just a little deeper, so you can understand how to apply it with your children. By focusing their *minds* on the process of reaching their goal and visualizing their success, the Russian athletes not only accomplished their goals, but also showed the greatest amount of improvement. This means that we have a much stronger *will* than we might think we have. It means our *will* can make our *way*. In fact, on a daily basis we can, just by thinking, picturing, and meditating on the path toward our success, somehow *train our brain* to find creative ways of reaching our goals before our feet ever even hit the ground.

Here Comes the Sun

Let me get practical here. Guide your children to an understanding that if they want to reach a certain goal, if they want to be a certain kind of person, they must "see" it in front of them. They must turn a blind eye toward all the negative nonsense the world projects in front of them. They must seek their own way out of the limiting cave we all begin in. They must take *active steps* out of that cave, toward the picture of their success. They have to be willing to confront the detractors. Yes, it takes time, it takes energy, it takes practice, and it takes fortitude. It takes encouragement from you as a parent, constantly reminding them of their power to unshackle themselves and, to paraphrase that old army slogan, *be all they can be*. It's also worth reminding you that it takes a readjustment period. Our children have to adjust to that light of knowing that they can actually get where they want to go.

Picturing the Final Product

When an artist wants to begin a sculpture, she first needs the tools (clay, a chisel, her hands). But that's not really enough, is it? She *then* needs some kind of a *vision* of what to sculpt. A picture in her head of what she wants this amorphous lump of clay to look like when she's done. If she wants to sculpt a giraffe, she'll use those tools to proceed, shaping the clay like the picture in her head. But the process will be different—she'll *use the same tools differently*—if she intends to turn the same lump into a flamingo.

In the same way, if an athlete wants to win big, he needs certain tools. He needs to know the rules of the game, the proper practices and techniques, the kind of conditioning necessary for success, and the lessons of the masters. Yet this is where people often stop. If they lack the *vision* that will direct their actions toward a specific achievement, our children are just going to wind up "playing" instead of winning. By definition, the whole point of visualization is to *envision* the process, to picture the end game, preferably with you in it, in clear detail. You can do this for yourself as you mentally prepare for the act of assisting your children on this journey. Then you can show them how to do the same for themselves.

For example, if your child's dream is to be a great golfer, he needs to have the tools and work on his skills. But ultimately he needs to *visualize* what he wants to achieve on the course. Only when you combine the kind of on-the-course physical practice with extensive visualization will you jumpstart your success. It only makes sense. Golfers become so adept at positive visualization that they report sometimes picturing their swing, the contact, the landing, all day long (sometimes to the consternation of their spouses!). They're setting themselves up for success. What if you were to just wander up to the ball and chop at it randomly, with no image in your head of how you wanted to swing, or where you wanted the ball to go? Can you predict the difference in the result? In short, visualization is a necessary element in achieving any goal or dream. If it works for Olympians, it can work for your children.

~

Little Kid, Big Imagination

You know this paradox has always struck me, that, as a rule, the younger the child, the bigger the imagination. What's that about? Well, before you learn what's possible and not, what's "real" and what's a "fairytale," you can't tell the difference, so it all looms large. The moon might be made of cheese. There might be elves in the forest. You might just be queen of all you survey, but as we "mature," we tend to shed those "childish things." And I guess this is good on the one hand. We all need to grow up. Someone has to work at air traffic control, and solve the hunger problem in Rwanda. Someone has to teach physics, and pave the highways. But have you ever noticed that once we do grow up, so many of us try desperately to go back to thinking imaginatively? Just look at how successful Disney and science fiction are with adults. Look at the success of Peter Pan and other stories of kids who never grew up. Look at amusement parks and videogames, and even pro sports to a great extent. The lesson is there are a few "childish things" worth salvaging. Imagination and belief are necessary for our sense of well-being.

So why do we have so much trouble maintaining our imagination? The problem is that as we grow up, the adults around us start to squash our fantasies in favor of "reality." Their goal is to mature us, but in many ways, they are limiting us. We learn to not trust our imagination and to question the validity of our dreams. You're *not* the queen of the frogs at the pond, you're taught. You're *not* the long-lost daughter of a wizard who will someday come to bestow on you your birthright. You're just Kelly Smith, a boring little pigtailed girl from south Detroit, with no mystical, magical, royal blood. The moon doesn't follow you in the back of the car. The wind isn't whispering secrets for only you to hear. In fact, nothing big and amazing is going to happen to you, so you might as well give up wishing. *That's* maturing? That's sad.

There must be a way that we as parents can give our children the tools to grow and mature, without stomping out their imaginations. The child that today dreams of being a fairy might tomorrow dream of being a polar explorer, and eventually dream of going to Yale or of teaching anthropology or doing missionary work in Nepal or cracking the cancer code—if we don't extinguish the furnace in her that sparks her dreams.

Sharpening the Tools of Visualization

Listen with your children to your favorite classical music and ask them what it makes them think of, what images come to mind as they listen.

Take your children on a walk through your neighborhood and encourage them to imagine what it was like a hundred years ago, a thousand years ago, and what it might be like in a hundred more years. Try to get them to flesh out details, and really picture things.

Take your children to an art museum and talk about the artwork. Ask them, "What do you think the artist was thinking when he made this?" "What does it make *you* think and feel?"

Encourage your children's imagine with "thought experiments" like, "What do you think is going on the dog's head right now?" and "What would happen if the dinosaurs came back tomorrow?"

Get your children in the habit of telling you about their nighttime dreams, or even writing them down regularly in a dream journal you can give them as a gift. Ask them to recount as best as they can the *sensory details*—what things looked like, felt like, sounded like, tasted like, even *smelled* like. Smell is the most primitive sense, and the one most closely bound-up with emotions. It's good to incorporate it as much as possible in positive visualization.

Raven's Vision

When Lydia and I were raising Raven and the eight Dream Catchers were taking shape in my consciousness, we began to come up with some simple exercises that would help our daughter keep that filmstrip of her dreams and imagination flipping through her consciousness.

A Five-Part Plan for Turning Vision into Reality

1. First, you have to help your children *clarify* their goals. The clearer the goal or dream, the better they can

visualize it. You can help them clarify with some probing questions aimed at getting them more detailed and specific: "When you say you want to be friends with Roger, what do you mean? What kind of stuff do you want to do together? What would it be like palling around with him? When you see yourself hanging out with him, where are you?" Or . . . "You say you would really love to get into boating. What kind of boat do you see yourself in? A motorboat? A kayak? When you picture it, are you with other people in the boat, or alone? Do you see yourself racing someone else? Or just floating peacefully somewhere?" You get the idea. This phase is pretty straightforward, yet many times it's one of the hardest obstacles to get past. Sometimes the dream will come into focus right away, as when Raven said, "I want to be on that show," and sometimes it will take some time and some massaging to coalesce into a clear picture.

As you help your children clarify their dreams, keep in mind that your role is not to limit or restrict, though you might sometimes need to redirect a bit.

2. In addition to questioning your children about their dreams, you can also *expand* their thinking by introducing them to various aspects of the dream state. If, for example, you discover that their dream is to become a doctor, you can ask their pediatrician to spend some time with them, talking about all the things she does. Maybe they can even shadow the doctor during some of her duties. You can subtly start introducing movies, books, and websites about medicine. I say "subtly,"

because parents must be careful not to inundate their children with the topic, which can backfire.

If you have a child interested in "flying," you can introduce all manner of flight-related new experiences, to continue to help refine the dream. Maybe their dream is to test-pilot new spacecraft—but maybe it's to study hawks and eagles. Maybe it's to design a more aerodynamic wing—but maybe it's to explore possible links between pterodactyls and chickens. You can get closer to defining the dream by bringing them to the air and space museum, the bird section at the natural history museum, a vista where you can see ultralight aircraft flying above, a hot air balloon festival, the launch pad for the space shuttle, a summer flight camp, a helicopter tour of a big city in your region, a landing zone for skydivers, a hill where birds of prey circle, even a movie about World War II pilots . . . the possibilities are endless. Doing activities like this will satisfy their craving and intensify their dreams. And soon it will begin to distill the specifics of their dream, the essence of what they're after. In the meantime, you've just had a hell of a time together with your children, and most of the activities haven't cost you a dime.

3. Now, you can help *insinuate* your children into the dream, using visualization. Help them to begin to picture their dreams in practice—in action—in their life. This takes some practice and some focus. If they want to be involved in fashion design, for example, sit down with them and get them visualizing *doing* fashion design.

Where do they see themselves? Is it drawing designs at a drafting table? Is it traveling the world buying exotic fabrics? Is it working with those fabrics to create a garment? Once they become involved in any way, get them to visualize the kind of success they want in every step. If they're starting to draft designs, help them visualize the final product as they want to see it. If they're submitting a design to a competition, help them picture themselves winning. You get the idea.

Once they get in the habit of visualizing, they can do so for every step. Before that big conversation with a friend. Before that oral presentation at school. Before the free throw. Everything we do is a kind of performance, so rehearsal—especially *mental rehearsal*—is vital for success.

4. You should encourage your children to *replicate* their visions as often and as vividly as possible. The key here is to consistently and continuously envision their dream. *Repetition leads to automation.* As they do this, they should focus on *positive* visuals, and focus on them as frequently as possible. If, as they visualize, they picture themselves again and again breaking the ribbon at the end of a big race, all their conscious action and behaviors—as well as their unconscious motivations—will lead them to that inevitability. Frequency of visualization is essential. This can't be an every-once-in-a-while thing.

5. Mental images should be *emotional.* They should think about people who have succeeded before them, imagine

the kinds of feelings success must have caused—and then try to *feel* them. If they're struggling with this, ask them to think about times when they did well, when they felt like they'd really nailed something, and then "dial up" that emotion, try to inhabit that state again while envisioning their future success.

Emotional "Muscle" Memory

Raven trained hard to get it right. She didn't lip-sync, she didn't flub her choreography, she learned her script lines quickly and seldom required multiple "takes." When it came time for a performance, she visualized the successes she experienced in rehearsal, picturing how it would look and feel. On stage, she *recreated* that vision, and usually performed to perfection.

You've probably heard of "muscle memory," which means your muscles, after having performed the same action again and again, begin to replicate that action without your having to *consciously* think about each step. You drill and drill and suddenly, it comes naturally. Well, I'm proposing there's such a thing as psychic memory, too, meaning if you picture it clearly, and feel the associated feelings, when it comes time to actually perform, your mind kicks your body into gear, and you're spot-on—or at least better than you would be without this mental practice.

Raven used her past successes not so much as an abstract model, but as an emotional and physical preparation for success. Because she spent her time in rehearsal visualizing her goal, her whole being was aware of what it needed to do to hit the right note, get every move of the dance routine down pat, and to say her lines clearly and authentically. Most important, she was *emotionally connecting* her experience during the performance with her successful rehearsal or past performance, allowing her to feel comfortable and confident. During those occasional times when her confidence was a bit shaky, I simply reminded her: "Hey, remember how quickly you learned those lines last week? You're a natural. You have an inbuilt talent for memorizing lines." And she'd smile and say, "Oh, yeah. I guess that was pretty easy. Oh, I can do that again."

The key is that smile. If you encourage your children to visualize success, but that vision lacks a *personal, emotionally tangible experience* to anchor to as a reference point, it is likely that the "performance" of whatever they wish to accomplish won't be as successful as it could be. It might feel "clinical," like going through the motions—or it might not happen at all. It's one thing to *picture* success, but without the emotional anchor, you might not get there.

Using a successful moment in your child's past such as when they scored the winning goal in a soccer game, or when they baked that incredible chocolate cake that everyone raved about, will help them understand what they're supposed to do in this process. Get your children feeling the tension, the thrill, and the fun of winning the game, of success. Those feelings will inspire them to relive that experience, or rather, re*discover* that feeling in a new exciting endeavor.

Once your children have started to get comfortable using their own past experiences as tools for visualization, they can begin to use their heroes and other role models as guides to visualizing their success. This might prove a challenge at first, but you need to remind your children that they are imagining the *feeling* of someone else's success. "What do you think that woman is feeling right now as she prepares to drop her board onto that half-pipe?" Or, "What must it feel like to act in that show?"

The positive emotional connection to the visual—and to the actual physical experience—is indispensable to future success, because those emotional connections activate little sensors inside of our minds. They trigger a flood of good-feeling chemicals. That's right—just like drugs do, but with none of the negative consequences. This allows us to transcend our fears and insecurities, to feel, in short, "high"—the kind of "natural high" that runners and other athletes and performers describe. Whenever we're in the zone of enjoying what we're doing and feeling as though we're doing well, we get that rush. And later, the craving for that feeling draws us back to the soccer field, or the stage, or the kitchen to create another amazing chocolate cake.

Visions Become Things

The message here is that our minds manifest our reality. I'll give you an example of this. My son, Blaize, was always playing videogames when he was younger. There was a particular game with a snowboarding theme. Although he had never actually snowboarded—it wasn't exactly big in Atlanta—he was crazy good at the video version, and he played constantly. I used to watch him play. I noticed how his emotions were so strong when he executed certain tricks, or landed the jumps right, and I marked how he put his whole body in the moves (this was before the days of Wii games where you actually have to use your whole body—in the "old days" all you really needed were your fingers on the buttons). We had had some conversations about whether or not the skills he'd built playing the snowboarding game would actually translate to the real slopes. I explained to him that before diving competitions in high school, I used visualization, replaying in my head what I would do to make the perfect dive, and asked him whether he thought he'd been doing essentially the same things on the videogame—mentally preparing to make those moves with his body.

So when he was twelve, we went snowboarding up at Big Bear. We started on the bunny slope, with me on skis and him on a snowboard. At first he fell a few times, but I could see him rapidly adapting and learning from every mistake. Then we tried the big slope. I said, "Just think about playing that videogame. Imagine you're in your room just killing at that game, totally mastering every move."

Bam! That did it. He was right beside me the whole time, whooshing down that mountain. He was performing moves he'd never actually physically done before, with respectable precision. It just seemed to happen naturally, like he had been doing it his whole life. And in a way, he had. His devotion to that game had paid off big time. The images of succeeding at that sport, and the emotions that came with it, had become a part of him. He could visualize how it was all supposed to work, and he could feel what it was supposed to feel like, having played this out so many times before in front of his TV screen. Now the final piece was in place, and his body was simply acting out what was in his mind.

I learned a lot from this. I learned that thoughts produce things, and visions produce things. The "mind" is so much bigger than the brain. The mind does not know time, and it doesn't know "impossible." So as you envision things, so they become. As soon as we humans grasp some vision in our mind—like curing a disease—our minds also start to manufacture that dream as reality. It leads us to the solutions, it brings us the people, moves us into the circumstances to make the dream come true.

People don't just "wind up" going to the moon. It takes a visionary like John F. Kennedy to imagine it as a reality, to picture it, then share it. Then look what happens. The vision inspires others, brings them together, assembles the will and the tools and the talent to make the dream a reality with a life of its own.

Finally, remember that negative visualization is formidable, too: If all you and your children picture are misery and failure, you will certainly find them. Sometimes we end up allowing ourselves to be shackled in those chains again, and only looking at the shadows.

One of the greatest gifts we can give our kids is this Dream Catcher of visualization, which promises that whatever their hearts and minds create as a dream can be made manifest. When we give them this gift, it lives on forever. Cultivating this habit will cut the chains off your children, and lead them in the real world of possibility, the real light of their greatest dreams. The sun will shine directly on them. Brilliant!

Dream Catcher Four

Aim Straight

If one advances confidently in the direction of one's dreams, and endeavors to live the life which one has imagined, one will meet with a success unexpected in common hours.

—Henry David Thoreau, American author

This Dream Catcher focuses on the idea that you need to train your children to *aim* for the future they want—to aim their efforts and attention toward their dreams. We must show them that if they expect to get somewhere, they need to know where that "somewhere" is. As adults, life is hard and the struggle often convinces us that it is easier to go with the flow; there's no point in wanting more than what we have, and that swimming upstream will exhaust us. If we've trained ourselves not to aim for our dreams in our own lives, we often fail to teach our children to aim for theirs. This Dream Catcher is designed to help you understand how to direct and focus children to put them on the right track toward their dreams. It will demonstrate that "aim" begins with the all-powerful *intention*, evolves into a sharp *focus*, then expresses itself through *action*, or taking *steps*, literally and figuratively, toward goals and dreams. I'll describe in detail how to introduce this idea to kids, how Raven and I used the technique, and how to sharpen the blades of aim regularly.

What Is Aim?

Very early on, we teach our children to aim for the toilet. We teach them to aim their fork for their mouth, their crayons inside the lines, their laundry for the hamper, the trash for the bin, the ball for the basket (and they seem to learn on their own to aim their dart guns and their water pistols at their siblings). Later, we teach them to aim their car inside the lane, so we don't lose them to oncoming traffic. And yet so many of us don't tell our children that they must aim for the *future* they want, they must aim their efforts and attention toward their dreams.

We might be reluctant to hammer home this lesson because we're afraid our children will be disappointed if they don't hit their target. Or maybe we want them to "play the field" instead of choosing a position prematurely. But I think we're just not used to aiming ourselves. Most of us never employed this strategy in our own youth, and many of us don't aim for our goals even in adulthood. We tend instead to drift, to "go with the flow," or blow with the prevailing winds. As a result, many of us would say we somehow wound up where we are, in our marriages, our jobs, our homes, for better or for worse. But how sad is that? How tragic! We blame circumstances, the boss, our upbringing, our color or creed, for where we are. But secretly, all of us know we're not rafts in the ocean. We're not dust in the wind. *The difference between us and the dust is that we can aim.*

If It's to Be, It's Up to Me

You can't wait around for the world to do something for you. It's never going to happen—no matter how much you want it to happen—unless you *make* it happen. That's a valuable lesson for our children. We can encourage our kids to think about aim and intention this way: Would you rather be lost at sea in a boat with oars, or without? Sure, the ocean itself will move you, but who can say which way? If you're lucky, perhaps to some paradise island. But more likely, into the Bermuda Triangle, or a place the old sailors know as Shark Reef. It's much better to keep your hand on the tiller, so that no matter which way the waves want to take you, you can steer right through, always heading in the direction you want to go. Inside all of us *is* such a rudder, an internal navigation unit that we can program for any direction. We must keep our hand on that tiller at all times, lest the currents carry us where they will, or a rogue wave swamps the little vessel that is our life. The achievement of children's dreams is not a function of randomness, but the result of intention.

Intention Is the Mother of Creation

"*I intend to. . . .*" We use this expression in everyday life, but what does the key word, *intention*, actually mean? What does it mean to *intend* to do something? And what does it mean when you either *follow through* with your intention—or don't follow through? If you don't wind up pursuing an original intention, was it ever a true intention in the first place? Or just an idea? It's important to teach your children the important role of intention in their lives. They must understand that intention is one of the most formidable tools in their arsenal. Properly sharpened, intention can catapult you pretty much anywhere. You won't win unless you first intend to win. You won't survive unless you intend to survive.

Intention is a constant and consistent focus on something you deeply desire, something you want to make happen. Intention is incredible. In fact, nothing can happen anywhere at any time without it. In most traditions, the very birth of a creation began with intention. Think: "Let there be light!" Now, I'm not a theologian or philosopher—and I definitely don't want to give you the impression that I'm preaching any particular faith—but this kind of thing really gets my juices flowing. This one simple statement that opens Genesis implies a complex series of *intentional* events. First, a *consciousness* ("Hey, I'm here, and I'm gonna look around"). Second, a *questioning* ("Hmm . . . is it kinda dark here, or it just me?"). Next, an *awareness* ("I definitely notice there's no light"). Then, a *dissatisfaction* with present circumstances ("You, know, it's too damn dark"). Following, a *will to change* the situation ("I really would like to *do* something about this darkness"). After that, a *recognition* of the options ("Some *light* would be nice, I think"). Subsequently, a *conviction* that change is within one's power ("*I* can *make* it light"). Penultimately, a *decision* ("Indeed, I *shall* make it light"). And finally, an *action* ("Light it up!").

In the case of this first Bible story, the action takes the form of a decisive "command" to the Universe. Even though your child is not God, regardless of your faith, you can still safely teach them that their intentions can be so strong— and so certain to succeed—that they can feel quite like commands to the Universe.

Naturally, we have to nurture our intentions. We can't *just* say, "Let there be an Academy Award for me!" Intention, for us, is just the start of creation, albeit a very powerful, very compelling start. Constant intention is necessary, like a "driving force," fueled by repeated reminders of your intention, until you reach its object, your dream.

Explain it to your children this way: Let's say we're sitting in a parked car in our driveway. Way on the other side of our state there's a theme park called Dreamland, a thousand times cooler than Disneyland, it's free to get in, and we can stay as long as we like. What should we do? Well, the average kid is going to know exactly what you should do: Get going! But here you can ask some questions to get them thinking about how intention works. "What do you mean, 'get going?' What do we have to *do* in order to 'get going?'"

We have to start the engine, we have to give the car gas, constantly, the whole time we're on our way. We have to steer the car, too, all the way, ever-closer to our intended destination. But most important, we have to know *where* we're going, otherwise all that gas and steering will be for naught. But interestingly, we don't have to know *exactly* where the place is, at least we don't need to know that to get started. All we really need to know as we leave the driveway is pretty much the right *direction* to go in. And even if we *don't* know the direction right away, we can always make some turns along the way—even U-turns!—if we find out we're getting off track. You can have a lot of fun with this analogy if you get creative. The message is: If you don't know where you're going—or you don't have any desire to go there— you're not leaving your driveway anytime soon.

Put another way, intention is *deciding to focus.* You can introduce this idea to your children like this: You know, people who wear glasses can't see where they're going very well unless they have their glasses *on.* Well, intention is kind of like that—it's your mind putting on a pair of glasses that allows you to see more clearly where you're going. And the best part about these glasses (let's call them "The Lenses of Intention") is that with them on, you see whatever you *want* to see in front of you—not someone else's idea of what *should be* in front of you (ideas discussed in "Dream Catcher Three: Picture It"). So whenever you find yourself seeing the world a little blurry (and maybe you're bumping into stuff) you can always polish up those glasses, put them on, see your intended future clearly, and go confidently in that direction. After a while, your eyes will adjust to those Lenses of Intention so well that you'll forget you even have them on. They'll become like *Contact* Lenses of Intention!

Intending to Party

When I was in high school, I had an amazing experience related to intention. I'm not sure I can get across how momentous this event was in shaping my views on intention, but I'm going to try.

Our house in Atlanta had a really interesting landscape, and from the upstairs, where I spent a lot of time, I used to look out and down at the terraced property, some cool boulders, and even a lake. One late afternoon as the sun was going down, I was on the back deck, and I suddenly pictured a party down there—a party *I* was hosting. It was extremely vivid and specific, this vision. And I decided right then and there that I would have this party. I resolved it. I *intended* to make it happen.

Now, I'd gone to some parties, but I'd never thrown one myself. At this point in my life, I had good friends, but I wouldn't really describe myself as "popular." I wasn't sure how my parents would react to the concept of my hosting a party. I didn't have any idea whether anyone would come. Still, I was determined to get this party thing on the agenda. As I focused on my intention, I realized that I wasn't even that interested in partying, so much as I was interested in the experiment: in experiencing my dream coming true.

Sure enough, it did come true. That May I hosted the blowout party of the season. It was *the bomb*. I'm not kidding—people still talk about that party to this day! The turnout was huge, just as I'd imagined. Everyone had a blast, just like in my vision. In fact, almost everything was exactly as I'd pictured it would be. I've delved into this phenomenon a lot more in Dream Catcher Three. But here, I want to call your attention to what I focused on that night in 1983. I didn't spend most of the party outside with the revelers. Instead, I was compelled to the room upstairs, and, looking out from the perch where I'd envisioned all this some months before, I was astounded. It was like déjà vu. There were the girls dancing to Funkadelic and Average White Band. There were the people by the sizzling barbecue. There were my friends hanging out on the rocks. I sat back and thought, "Damn, that's exactly what I wanted." And then I thought, *Holy s**t, I made this happen.* It was so surreal, and the impression so strong, that it still lingers in me, thirty-something years later. It was my first taste of the reliability of my own intentions. *If I could get this done*, I remember thinking, *then I can do . . . well—anything I set my mind to.*

Forcing the Issue

People ask me sometimes whether I "forced" Raven into doing the things she did on the way to success. Aside from the obvious question—how exactly do you force a kid to make a movie with Eddie Murphy and a bunch of cool animals, or star on the most popular show on the Disney Channel?—it's a valid question. Parents in particular when employing the Dream Catcher principles are concerned about forcing their own will on their children's dreams, and sometimes they wonder where the line is between what their children desire for themselves and what they want for their children. Big surprise! That's what all parents go through, all the time. But the answer is simple. Sometimes, you've just got to apply force. Period. For example, when you insist that your children go to school, you're enforcing your will. When you make them go to bed, come home early, clean their room, finish their homework, what do you think you're doing but forcing them? Without your guidance, they will often not know what they're doing. In the worst-case scenario, they could make very bad decisions for themselves.

Even if they told you where they wanted to go, could they get there on their own? They depend on you for special direction. By following your example, children slowly build the skills, the self-awareness, and the confidence to walk their own path.

okay, let me take it back—let's not call it "forcing." Let's call it "cajoling." If your child is wonderfully talented in gardening or windsurfing, farming or fundraising, and they one day announce they want to quit, you have to show them the wisdom and the rewards of perseverance and persistence, discipline and stick-to-itiveness.

INTENTIONS ARE *BELIEFS IN ACTION*

In addition to my visualizations, my intentions reached their mark. Intentions are fueled by our awareness of them, our acknowledging them, and speaking them to the world. They are like oaths we make to ourselves, promises to the Universe from our spirits. And the intention somehow sends out streams of energy to the Universe, and starts to create a chain reaction of what we might call circumstances (if such a thing exists): The right people and opportunities come along at the right time, and right when you're ready. You're on your way to achieving your goal.

Intention is an important Dream Catcher because without it, nothing happens, or if something does happen, it seems random and unplanned (it's actually not random; you just intended for nothing particular to happen). A party is not an accident. It's not something that just "happens." You have to intend it. So, too, with a career in nursing, a cross-country walk, a Boy Scout knot. These things don't happen without intention. And neither will your children's dreams.

Knowing When to Push

I have a story about my son, Blaize, that makes me think about this issue of cajoling. I'd given up clarinet in high school, but somehow passed on the musical gene to Blaize. At age five, he was already pretty good at the piano. I thought this talent would serve him well in life. He'd always have the joy of music, and he could become a concert pianist some day, or a synthesizer player in a huge band, or he could always open his box, and someone would put money in there. But we allowed him to stop when he told us he wanted to quit. Well, maybe keyboards just weren't for him. Maybe he was bored. Maybe the Universe and his spirit were shouting at him to do something else with his life—he's a damn good athlete, for sure. But looking back, I regret letting him give up the piano so easily. I think he would have been awesome now at seventeen, a regular Stevie Wonder.

I think it's our responsibility as parents to push our kids further than they're at first willing to push themselves. That goes without saying, I suppose. We wake them up and get them dressed and make them eat and shove them out the door to go to the bus stop . . . but we're afraid of forcing them to play piano for a few more months, maybe the only few months it might take for them to break through some barrier and become great?

You can explain to your children that once you decide on your goal, you've got a strong intention. Now you aim for that goal, and make sure every step gets you closer to that direction. Once you start moving, there's something called the energy of momentum. A snowball rolling downhill keeps rolling, gets faster, and becomes larger, stronger, and more solid. In the same way, aiming toward our intention— to conquer our fear of walking to school alone, to donate our hair to Locks of Love, whatever it is—makes it harder to stray off course. But if you see your children are weaving a bit off their course, you've got to step in to bump them in the right direction. You obviously don't *violently force* them. You encourage them. You hearten them, cheer them, remind them of the goal. You say, "Trust me. You'll make it. Hang in there. The destination's right around the corner."

Every once in a while, you might want to encourage a short break from the aim toward the dream. Sometimes we need a little perspective, and it's helpful to slow down to see it. Sometimes we want to stop and enjoy the view.

And sometimes, you might have to really listen to find out whether your children really don't want to pursue a particular dream anymore. Even then, you can try to determine whether they're really giving up or just in a slump. You can find out the core problem and see if there's a way to fix it.

Find ways to make the journey toward the dream more fun, more desirable. Diversify the steps to get there. Shake it up. If your children are doing laps every day, they're going to get bored. So change up the routine and do some cross-training. Or change the venue.

If they truly begin to consistently and strongly resist the pursuit of the dream, then their intention has probably changed. Their visions have changed. Their beliefs have changed. So you can try to aim them all you want toward a certain goal, but they're never going to get there. Now you will be "forcing" it. Time to start over, and work on exploring and clarifying a new dream. Welcome to parenting.

A Toddler's Intention Makes Rain

Stephanie Austin, founder of Atlanta's Young Faces modeling agency, "discovered" Raven-Symoné in Atlanta in 1986. By "discovered," I mean she recognized what Raven already knew about herself, and had certainly convinced us: She was going to be a star. Stephanie believed it wholeheartedly, and that belief further encouraged all of us. The belief morphed into the intention in all of us, to help get her to her goal. As you know, Raven knocked it out of the park at Young Faces, and got a lot of local and regional work. After a year, Stephanie believed Raven could go much further, and encouraged me and Lydia to take Raven to New York for the all-important and super-competitive "commercial season," during which Stephanie believed the opportunities would abound for Raven.

We all intended to make that journey, take those steps, to make it happen. You see, belief coupled with a plan of action put into play equals intention. Stephanie's belief in Raven's talents got us the hook-up with her friend at the top agency in New York, and soon we were sitting at an interview with Barbara Laga, director of the children's division at the prestigious Ford Modeling agency. Ford Models have included Christie Brinkley, Elle MacPherson, Cheryl Tiegs, and Twiggy. It was no joke.

Barbara believed in a big future for Raven, too, and intended to make her a huge success. She signed Raven based on that belief and intention, and Raven became one of the agency's youngest talents. Everyone who worked with Raven in New York believed she was going to blow up. In part because she was so charming and adorable, not to mention professional and poised. But mainly because she exuded confidence: Her belief in herself and her dream of landing that big show were infectious. We all held onto that intention, and soon we went from pounding the pavement on cold calls and open auditions to getting invitations to meet top art directors, producers, and people in casting.

Raven started to book national TV and print ads as Barbara intended, and held onto that plan to get on *Cosby*. Her "big break," of course, was finally meeting Bill Cosby, who also believed in her future—so much so she was signed with Carsey-Werner Productions to play the role of "Olivia Kendall." She was still only three years old. That's the power of intention, and it can work for your children, too. The key is to pay attention to what they're expressing as a dream, assess whether it's really serious, whether it's gotten a foot-hold in their soul—then show them that belief can turn into reality through the vehicle of intention.

~

Failure Is Not a Fact

When it comes to teaching our children aim and intention, people often ask me, "But what if my kids fail? Then what? Isn't it bad to get them dreaming and focused if it can all lead to a huge disappointing failure?" It seems like a good question, but it contains an inherent fallacy. It assumes there is such a state as "failure." Now you might say, "Of course there's such a thing as failure. You can't have *intention* without the possibility of missing your intended mark, right?" If you start out in Alabama, aim for California, but wind up in Arizona, you've failed in your mission, haven't you? Well, let's explore that.

Failure is a state of mind, not a fact. It's all in your head. It depends on how you look at your circumstances. But, you might say, *Arizona is not a state of mind—it's a state of the Union, and one decidedly east of California, your intended destination. So how is that not a failure? How is that all in my head?* Here's how. Although Arizona is not California, it's a hell of a lot closer to California than Alabama, where you began. So . . . you've just learned that you haven't failed, you just *haven't succeeded yet.* You're not at your destination because you have to keep going forward to get there. This simple paradigm shift in your brain can prevent the onslaught of negative feelings and self-recrimination that come from "accepting defeat."

Another technique you can teach your children is to simply learn from mistakes and missteps. When your son's team loses a game, instead of allowing him to get depressed and weep, "Oh, we lost, we lost!"—a negative state of mind that will adversely affect his body and his emotions tremendously—help alter his thinking by asking him what he learned from the experience. Get him going along this path, instead: "Maybe I need to practice my defense, or bone up on jump shots and free throws. Maybe I need to adjust my stance, or concentrate better." It's amazing what can happen when you just change the concept in his mind, where "failure" or "intended success" reside.

Always Add Action to Aim

Remember that all the aim and intention in the world will prove ultimately fruitless if you don't get your butt in gear. I once heard a hokey—but true—analogy along these lines, from the world of baseball coaching: *You can't steal second if your foot is still on first.*

When Raven was four, she started to talk about wanting to sing. I could tell the dream was serious when she brought it up all the time, and when she started focusing on singers on TV and the radio. So whenever we went anywhere in the car, we played our favorite sirens on CD: Chaka Khan and Miki Howard. As the music played, we looked in the rear-view mirror and saw intense concentration on Raven's face.

She was listening and absorbing. And then she started singing along. Of course we strongly encouraged this. After all, if you want to be an amazing singer, you could do worse than trying to emulate Chaka Khan!

Every opportunity we had to get Raven singing, we took it. Every time she sang, she got closer to her dream.

With Limited Time, Aim for the "Vital Few"

When it comes to aim and focus, we have to remember to consider the finite amount of time our children are allotted to accomplish their goals. The 80/20 Principle is a useful tool for helping them maximize the time they spend pursuing their dreams, especially when the competition for their attention is so great. It works particularly well for mature kids. Try explaining it this way: Not everything in the world is equal, you know that. The secret of life is to approach your tasks with that mindset: Determine the few things that do matter, then do them consistently and do them well—and stop doing the things that don't matter, or at least spend a lot less time on them. This is cool because it actually frees up a huge amount of time (because right now you're probably spending about 80 percent of your time doing stuff that doesn't get you closer to what you want). When you reinvest even part of that 80 percent of your time back into the stuff that *does* matter (about 20 percent of all the stuff you do), you'll get enormously better at just those things (the only things that matter), and you'll succeed much faster—get better grades, make more money when you're older, and so on—even as you've freed up lots of time. Most successful people in the world employ this strategy every day, to everything they do.

Only one question will start you off on this process: How do you decide what's in your vital 20 percent? Well, you ask yourself, "What do I want? What kind of life do I want? What do I want to accomplish? What is my mission in life?" You see, if you wish to be a great Arctic explorer, then doing well in science class will matter a lot more to you than practicing the piano. If your greatest wish is to go to the school dance with the quarterback, then playing fifty hours of All Star Cheer Squad on your Wii is not the most valuable use of your time. If, on the other hand, you want to be a cheerleader (or a world-class gamer) then go for it!

~

We cut Raven's first album, *Here's to New Dreams*, when she was only four. When it was released, people liked it, but it didn't sell hugely. It didn't go platinum. I can see how some people might call that a failure to launch into the music career Raven intended. But none of us saw it that way. Instead, we thought: Well, we wanted to make an album, and we made a good one. We did it. We got in the game and finished it. How many billions of people in the world never get that opportunity in a lifetime (about 6.75 billion, actually), no less when they're still a little kid. And, actually, the album spawned two successful singles, one of which made it onto the Billboard Hot 100. We also studied the sales, the critics, the listeners, and we learned how to do certain things better.

Raven did a second album, *Undeniable*, in 1999, which sold better than the first, but still not the hundreds of thousands we wanted (Raven and I had both intended to make her a platinum-seller). But we congratulated ourselves again, and we learned again, though we never looked backward.

Was I supposed to tell Raven that she'd "failed" as a recording artist? Did I want my child to think she couldn't sing well, that she wasn't good enough? Hell, no! Instead we told her: Hey, you're making music, and having fun, and getting paid, and gaining experience, and building a fan base, and all of that is the definition of success. We did the best we could with what we had—and it was good, if you ask me!—and we set it as a benchmark, knowing next time we'd do even better. We were in that metaphorical Arizona still, and we could see California over the border.

Later, Raven did some songs on the *Cheetah Girls* (2003) and *That's So Raven* (2004) soundtrack albums, which were certified gold for sales over 500,000 copies. When the *Cheetah Girls* album went platinum, we realized that her huge success was in large part based on the journey we'd already taken. The seeds for that success were sown in the earlier albums, when we were building all that experience, those skills, that listenership. Back when we started, had we been caught up in the idea of "failure," we might have stopped altogether, unplugged the mic, and packed it in.

You can apply this same line of thinking to your children's steps toward achieving their dream, regardless of the scale. Don't let them sink into failure mode. If they don't get the part they want in the summer camp production of *Grease*, they haven't failed. Even if they *get* the part, but they don't perform as well as they wanted to do—they haven't failed. These experiences some label as "failure" are simply part of the process; bumps on the road to success. These experiences shape us, harden us, build us up, and make us who we eventually become.

The secret is not to give up. Sounds simple, but that's it.

It's easier to avoid the state of mind called failure if you're continuing to *move and improve*. It's hard to believe that you've failed to arrive in California if you're actually still driving west—especially if you're already in western Arizona! So, finally, it's hard to believe in the concept of failure if you're still actively working toward success. Encourage your children to continue practicing, keep striving, keep dreaming.

The Good, the Bad, and the Intended

So now we have established that the expression "I intend" does not comprise mere throwaway words. Its force is staggeringly strong. Its initial utterance—and one's subsequent, vigilant attention to its follow-through—sets in force a kind of motion that is unstoppable. Here's intention in action for you: On February 10, 2007, a self-described inexperienced, improbable long-shot stood in the shadow of the old Statehouse in Springfield, Illinois, to announce his intention to become the next president of the United States. That speech sends shivers down my spine when I reread it or listen to it on

YouTube. It's a mind-blowing, audacious speech, especially in hindsight: You can see clearly through Obama's humility and innocence that he really *intended* to win, and would accept no other result. He quotes a predecessor, "a tall, gangly, self-made Springfield lawyer"—a very clever analogy on so many levels—and sets in motion a ripple in the way things *were*. The ripple becomes a wave, the wave an unstoppable tsunami, and nothing will ever be the same again. Whatever your political persuasion, it's clear that the most unlikely candidate trounced all the competition, just as Lincoln improbably saved the Union and freed a people when the odds were stacked against him.

I always believed that I never got sick, and the reality followed that strong belief: I didn't get sick. But that's not the whole story. After the belief came the intention. I intended to stay healthy, so I did. I intended for Raven to get on *Cosby*, to make albums and movies, and later, to get her own show. Raven intended these things for herself, too. Intention is a forward-moving state of mind, whereas belief can remain static. Intention propels you forward because it's bound up with a plan, with steps to turn belief into truth. Intention is like *belief in action*.

Pulling Focus

Focus is an important aspect of aim and intention. Just as a camera lens can focus on a far-distant object, so too can the mind focus on its dream as well as the immediate tasks at hand. What exactly does *focus* mean, and how do you achieve it? Well, focus is the total concentration on one thing—in this case, a dream. Try explaining it to your children this way: Think of a magnifying glass. If you tilt it the right way in the sun, it causes heat and eventually fire on the spot where it's focused. We are the same as that lens. We have the ability to create a spark that turns into an inferno, if only we tilt ourselves (aim the lens) toward the right spot, and we don't waver. Be that magnifying glass whenever you can. Focus your light. Intensify your intention. If we are able to exclude all things out of our minds, and focus directly on our end results, we can sail on that beam of light toward our goal, and burn it up when we hit that spot.

Filtering Out the Junk

It's difficult nowadays for young people to focus, because that level of concentration requires them to exclude the extraneous junk that overruns them, like peer pressure and TV. There are a few techniques you can use to help your children tune in to their inner voice.

First, you can ask your children to take time out—establish a set time—where there should be nothing but true focus. Establishing a specific time to practice and focus on the dream is important because it gets you and your children in the habit of making the time and giving over the time. It reminds you that it often takes discipline—not just desire—to accomplish something. If carving out large blocks of time proves challenging, try smaller bites of time, with a specific goal for each block of time. For example, if the dream is to get a poem published in the school literary magazine, you could schedule a fifteen-minute block of time on Saturday morning, with the only goal being to sit quietly and decide on the theme of the poem: *Do you want to write about the ocean? Love? A turkey sandwich?* Then on Sunday, you can schedule twenty minutes to write as many first lines of poems as you can think of based on the theme. On Monday before school, for ten minutes, the plan could be to describe the feeling of "coldness" without using the word *cold* or any word like it. On Tuesday before bed, you could set aside half an hour to pick your favorite first line, then write one next line that continues that mood. . . .

The goal of this process is fourfold: to get in the habit of setting a time to pursue what's important to you, to learn to focus during that set time, to increase the time gradually, and to increase the focus gradually.

Second, you can help your children begin to focus during their practice or "dream-fulfillment" time. During this time, say an hour a day (or more), they should focus in thought and in *deed* on the task at hand. If the dream is to submit a project to the state science fair, then they should work as diligently as possible on that project during this time. They should review past winners, talk to teachers, read science books, and search the Internet for cool stuff that will help them. They should use this time to study the rules of submission, and the criteria for winners. They should learn who the judges are, and what kind of experiments excite them. They should build a team of resources—people, most of all—to help them achieve their goal. And they should, of course, build their project.

Focus tends to be self-sustaining. Once you start, you get caught up, and you focus even more. If your children find themselves distracted, they can try a simple tactic for getting back on track. They should say to themselves, as time and motion expert Brian Tracy recommends: "*Back to Work.*" That usually does it.

Third, you can help your children with discipline in general. Any activity that requires periods of intense concentration—including videogame playing—trains your children for a future of focus. So play chess. Do puzzles. Share riddles with them that they have to ponder intensely.

Fourth, even during "free time," you can help your children work on focusing their dreams. In fact, it's a strange paradox that when we're most relaxed (something we'll delve into more soon) we're most susceptible to suggestions we give ourselves that can move us toward our dreams. So incorporate talk about the dream into whatever other activities you're doing. If the goal is to paint a giant mural on the side of the building to cover up the graffiti, you can bring up the subject while you're walking or driving together, or on the subway, or waiting at the doctor's office, or hiking through the park. In fact, if you catch your children in a mellow, meditative, seemingly unfocused state, you're likely to get them at their most receptive.

Whenever possible, incorporate positive visualization exercises, which you can review in "Dream Catcher Three: Picture It."

You're Getting Sleepy. . . .

In order to help your children aim and focus their intention, you can learn and then teach them relaxation techniques, which have proven to reduce anxiety and increase focus, inner peace, and performance in both children and adults. There are multiple methods and lots of resources available on the Internet and in the bookstore, but the procedures all share similar steps. Below is just a sample to get you started. Remember that *everyone* is open to these methods; you just have to be willing to submit to relaxation and to peace. Following is a script your children can use to relax themselves. You can introduce them to each step, and show them how to do it for themselves.

—— GETTING YOUR KIDS TO SLOW DOWN ——

It can be challenging to convince motivated children who rarely enjoy sitting still to make meditation part of their path to their dreams, but emphasizing its practical application and positive results will help it feel less esoteric for them. Of course, leading by example can also go a long way toward helping your child understand its relevance. Try making meditation a daily or weekly part of the entire family's routine. Or, explore options for a weekend-long youth meditation camp where your children will see the benefits of cultivating this type of inner focus—and that it's not only for adults!

1. Before you begin, think carefully about what you want to accomplish. Do you want more confidence as a public speaker? Do you want to hone your go-kart skills? Do you want to be less shy? Whatever your goal, clarify and articulate it in a few (one to three) brief and clear statements. These "suggestions" you will make to your subconscious should be framed in the present and the positive: It's better not to say, "I don't want to miss the ball when it comes toward me," but instead to say, "I move effortlessly toward the ball and block every goal." Other suggestions:
   - "I am confident and happy around other people. I like to meet new friends."
   - "I learn new guitar riffs easily and play them beautifully."
   - "I remember what I've learned, and have fun proving that on tests."

2. Sit or lie down comfortably in a quiet, not-too-bright room where you won't be disturbed. Turn off the TV and your cell phone. Don't cross your legs. Plan for 20 minutes to an hour.

3. Shut your eyes and relax. Tell yourself gently that you are relaxed, comfortable, happy, and receptive. This will help melt away any lingering stress, fear, or anxiety from your day.

4. Breathe slowly and deeply, and concentrate only on your breathing for a while. Whenever any other thought creeps into your consciousness, just think about your breathing, in and out, in and out. (This step alone is the basis for many meditative techniques, and you can use

it whenever you're feeling stressed, frightened, angry, or even depressed. After you've practiced it for a while, you can induce a state of deep relaxation within just a minute.)

5. Starting with the top of your head, try to be as conscious as possible of each part of your body, one part at a time. As you think about and feel your scalp, tell yourself gently to relax the muscles. We hold a huge amount of tension in our heads, which causes headaches, migraines, and all kinds of other unpleasantness. After you're certain the top of your head is relaxed, mentally picture moving down to your forehead, and relax those muscles, too. Keep going downward, identifying each part of your body (the brow, the nose, the cheeks, the jaw, the ears, the neck, the shoulders, etc.). As you recognize each part of your body, really try to *feel* it. As this deep physical relaxation slowly washes over you from the top, down—and as you have effectively cleared your mind of superfluous stresses—you will begin to feel very relaxed. You're approaching a state of meditation or self-hypnosis.

6. When you're completely done with every part of your body, ending with your toes, mentally re-check yourself, as sometimes small amounts of tension will have rebuilt, especially in the head and neck. Relax those muscles again.

7. It often helps to give yourself verbal suggestions. Say to yourself gently, "My neck is completely relaxed. My fingertips are completely relaxed." You can also use visualization. For example, you might want to imagine that

a warm radiance is emanating through your body from within, or warm, soothing water is seeping around your body, slowly relaxing every part of your body. Some people find it works to think of themselves gently sinking, floating, or softly falling. Maybe you can picture that you're on a slow escalator going down into a misty pool in which you can breathe. It also helps to think about soothing colors.

8. Enjoy this state of relaxation a moment. Revel in it. At this point, you are open to your inner voice. Anything you say to yourself at this point with conviction and repetition will take a firm hold in your subconscious. So this is when you begin to repeat to yourself the suggestions you formed earlier. It helps to repeat them slowly and confidently as many times as you wish. "I am patient and kind with animals, I am patient and kind with animals. . . ." After a while, you can switch statements, and move on to the next one. "I am at one with my horse when we ride, I am at one with my horse. . . ."

9. If you want to, you can combine these suggestions with visual imagery. For example, you can picture that you're floating in a warm, deep, cobalt blue sea. Every once in a while, a friendly dolphin swims up to you, and the dolphin gives you the suggestion. Or maybe you can be an astronaut, untethered and floating in space. Each beautiful, bright planet you encounter gives you an enormous gift you've been craving: peace, balance, joy, love . . . be creative. It's also valuable to try to experience the emotions associated with the suggestions and the imagery. If you're telling yourself

that you are graceful on the ice, picture those graceful moves, and *feel graceful.*

10. When you first begin this practice, you will likely find yourself occasionally distracted. This is normal. The meditative state is not like sleep. In fact, you are "hyper-aware" of what's going on around you. If a car alarm goes off, you *will* notice it. But you have the power to redirect your mind toward your suggestions, or toward your breathing. Others will find themselves falling asleep somewhere in the middle of this practice. This can be a welcome result if, like many adults and an increasing number of children, you have trouble falling asleep because of a racing mind. But the point is not to lull yourself to sleep. If you find yourself nodding off, concentrate again on the suggestions or the breathing.

11. Rather than just leaping up after your session, it's best to come out of your relaxed state gradually. Again, a visual image helps, such as riding an elevator up, or ascending a golden spiral staircase. With each step, you're getting closer to complete wakefulness.

"Multipotentiality"

In 1994, researchers studying gifted and talented children coined a fancy name for a rather wonderful dilemma: They called "multipotentiality" what we know as a child with several competing talents and interests. Just as Raven expressed interest and talent in both acting and singing, these children are interested in, and good at, several things—sometimes wildly divergent things, such as writing sonnets, building model rockets, and student government. While it seems like the kind of problem any parent would want for their child, it can lead to challenges when it comes time for the child to choose a focus. The researchers gave this an extravagant name, as well: "overchoice syndrome." My cowriter Ian's niece, Hannah, faced this challenge. When she was little, she loved and excelled at both dance and karate. For several years, Hannah's father, Mitchell, carted her from dance lessons to martial arts training. It wasn't until one of those talents—karate—kicked into full force that dance began to fall by the wayside. This was a natural and easy life transition for Hannah. Her sensei recognized her talent early, and made her choice relatively easy. "Non-quitting spirit" is one pillar in the character-building that goes along with the physical training at Hannah's dojo. She still enjoys dancing, and she's still one of the best kids on the stage—but she's a second-degree black belt in karate at age twelve. Karate has taken precedence in her mind and in her practice.

Hannah was lucky. Psychologists warn that when the interest, motivation, and opportunity are relatively equal for two or more dreams, children often suffer, even to the point of clinical depression. You can help your children evolve a focus on one main area of interest, a "primary dream," then follow through accordingly, using the questions in the "Whim or Dream?" section of "Dream Catcher One: Pay Attention."

~

I hope that after reading this Dream Catcher you'll be able to help your children filter out all the conflicting messages they receive about which direction to go in. With your guidance, your children can learn to focus on the destination of *their* dream, taking the best path—the one you lay out for them.

Dream Catcher Five

Get Real

There is no reality except the one contained within us.
That is why so many people live such an unreal life. They
take the images outside them for reality and never allow
the world within to assert itself.

— Hermann Hesse, German-Swiss poet, novelist, and painter

Even when you and your children are pursuing fantastic dreams together, you need to "keep it real." It's necessary to take stock of certain realities—financial, physical, geographic, and so on—and incorporate them into your plan for your children. The healthy way to do this is to recognize certain pragmatic realities as mere "bottlenecks" that must be overcome on the way toward dream-fulfillment—not as brick walls and total restrictions. Positively assimilating natural challenges and limits into your children's action plan for achievement is what I mean by "getting real." Part of this means understanding what success looks like. After all, if your children are aiming for the stars, the moon is still a dream come true. And if not the moon, the journey up is an accomplishment in and of itself. Here, we'll discuss how to invest children in the *process* of pursuing their dreams so that every real-world outcome is *positive* and not disappointing. Finally, we'll look at how to help your children get real emotionally.

What's the Deal with Getting Real?

First, we have to "Get Real" about the fact that it won't be easy. It took Raven many, many years to achieve her dream of getting her own show. And along the way, there were some false starts, some impediments, and some definite disappointments. The key is that she never gave up.

Rather than encouraging our children to move forward, we can sometimes unwittingly kill their dreams by promoting a "normal," "reasonable," "real" life, instead of a "fantasy." This is not what I mean when I urge you to Get Real.

Having said that, you've probably noticed that the moment you became a parent, certain "real" struggles and challenges immediately became apparent. Maybe you have to work fifty hours a week at a job you don't like in order to feed your family, or you have to travel more than you expected in order for your child to make all of the geography bees they want to compete in. These are just a few of the realities of parenting, and it is our job to assimilate these challenges into the daily work of raising our children to believe in themselves and their dreams.

So, to be clear, I'm not saying that you should simply nod and smile, and tell your children, like Pollyanna, "That's great. You can do it," to whatever they throw your way in terms of goals. You have to confront reality in this process. So, say your child comes to you and says, "I want to be a senator." "okay," you should respond. "That's doable. But you need to understand the realities that come with becoming a political leader." I mean the logistical, pragmatic realities. By way of helping your child digest these realities, perhaps you can download some great political speeches together, or take him to a rally during election time. Maybe you can visit the state senate chamber together, or arrange for a meeting with a local politician. You can help him work on his public speaking skills, his civics knowledge, and so on.

Most of all, you must communicate with your children. I can't stress this enough. When your child comes home from school and tells you, "The kids made fun of me when I said I wanted to be a lumberjack," you need to be ready to confront not only your child's bad feelings this might have occasioned, but the real fact that there will be more people along the road who will share similar disapproval of your child's dreams. Using this Dream Catcher, you can instill in your children a spirit of confidence, perseverance, and self-belief that will shine through every adversity and shut up the pessimism of the inevitable naysayers.

Let's focus on getting real with the day-to-day tasks of moving forward, and let's take stock of certain realities—financial, physical, geographic, academic, and so on—and incorporate them into our plan for our children. You can sit down with your family with a pen, a sheet of paper, and a good attitude, and work on a precise game plan, encompassing and integrating your challenges.

Get Real with Your Finances

This is a biggie. I have seen a lot of children's dreams crushed because of a perceived lack of funds. It's ingrained in us that "money makes the world go 'round," so it's easy to let our financial fears and responsibilities put a damper on our children's dreams. Especially in globally tough financial times like these, there aren't many of us who haven't been touched by recession. But I've learned several easy solutions for dealing with the stress monster of money, each of which will help you lay the financial groundwork for attaining your children's dreams. The first step is to truly, legitimately, I mean *really* get real about your budget. The vast majority of us underestimate the actual amount of money we're spending. So step one is to make a budget.

A Simple Family Budget

1. Write out a list of all your expenses, starting with your most basic needs like housing, food, and health care. Remember loans and credit cards. Look over your bank statements, your checkbook, and your online payments, to remind yourself of all your expenses.
2. Don't forget "hidden" expenses (parking fees, tips, birthday gifts, school books, and so on). An online budget calculator can help. The good ones include all kinds of expenses you're encountering without realizing them, monitoring them, and incorporating them in your budget (haircuts, for example).

   For sixty days, have every family member keep every receipt for every expense, no matter how small. Every stamp, ever highway toll, every snack you buy at the airport. Record them all at the end of each day on a calendar. Do this together. It's a simple way to become aware of your spending habits (to literally become accountable), to find things you could cut, and to teach your children a valuable lesson about responsible spending.

3. Now, tabulate all the expenses for the two months, and adjust your budget according to this reality. Remember that one-time expenses, such as annual tune-ups and taxes, need to be counted and spread out over each month.

4. With your real expenses now in front of you, you can work on finding places to cut back. It might become obvious that you're spending too much on dinners out, or on entertainment. It's okay to do these things once in a while—just budget them in, and stick to what you've budgeted. It's when you're blind to what you're spending that you tend to spend more indiscriminately. Now, make your own coffee and lunch at home instead of buying it out. Carpool. Cut out cable channels you never watch.

5. Cut out debt. Debt is a huge stressor, and prevents us from feeling free to change locations, get involved in new projects, and help our children achieve their goals. Not to mention it's a vicious cycle. The interest rates are usually so high that you'll never get out from under if all you do is send in the minimum payments. Make sure you budget money to pay down debt before you spend that money on unnecessary things. If you want more strategies to do this, use a not-for-profit (*not* a fee-based!) debt counseling service.

6. Cut out the expense of arbitrary clothing, toy, and food shopping that we so often do just to kill time, and spend that time together as a family, walking, talking, or helping your children practice violin or speed skating. If you use spending to feel good about yourself and make your problems go away, get help for that, because it's not the solution.

7. Save! Start putting away as much money as you can to build a cushion for disaster and a nest egg for the future. Economists call this paying yourself first, and there's wisdom in it. You should consider trying to build a more liquid emergency fund that you can get to in case of disaster. In the best-case scenario, you can budget for the things you will need to do to help your children get to their dreams (money for coaches, travel, special equipment, etc.): the Dream Catcher Fund.

8. Include your children in some of these discussions and decisions. Don't shield them from the reality of money, so that they grow up believing that it falls out of the sky when they need something. Tell your children how much you earn and how much you spend as a family. If your children are old enough, it's also not a bad idea to find ways they can contribute financially to their dream-fulfillment. If an upcoming band camp trip costs $1,000, what's wrong with telling them you expect them to chip in $100 by paying them for special chores, or by expecting them to get a part-time job that doesn't drastically cut into their practice time?

9. Consider supplementing your income. If you're serious about supporting your children's dreams full-on, then

you might need to earn more to do it. There's a balance here, of course, because you don't want your employment to take up all the time you could be spending with your children (ultimately, your time is worth more to them than your money, assuming a base-level of financial stability). I'm just thinking of Tiki Barber, the former Giants running back. His mother, with no external help, raised him and his brother Ronde (who plays for the Tampa Bay Buccaneers), working multiple jobs just to put food on the table and a roof over their heads. But this burden did not stop Geraldine from encouraging her sons to pursue their dreams of becoming NFL stars. She scheduled her various jobs in a way that enabled her to attend all of Tiki's games. I'm not saying it's easy—just that it's possible. Your children's dream-fulfillment is our goal here—not your breaking the bank. If your financial goals are aligned with your children's needs, both you and your children will grow closer together as your family gets closer to a dream fulfilled.

Get Real about the *Value* of Money

Lydia and I always stressed the *value* of money to Raven, even when she was little. We also helped her understand that while what she was doing was fun, it was also a job. That means you *get stuff you want when you do a good job.* So if Raven needed to learn lines for a show, we asked her what she wanted when she got those lines down. Let's say she wanted a "Hello Kitty" doll. Well, we hyped her up like crazy about getting that doll, to the point where she was sure to know her lines. Come taping day, she was excited and ready. She understood the connection between what she did and what she got, and that's a lesson we were proud to teach her, knowing that many parents wait to teach that lesson until it's almost too late.

I remember once when we came out to L.A. from New York for an appearance on *The Arsenio Hall Show*, and the whole mission was: Do a great job and you can go to the Hello Kitty store in the mall afterward. Raven did the show, sang a song, nailed the interview, had a great time, and by the time we were getting in the car, she was saying, "That was so cool. And now I get to go to Hello Kitty!" That was it. She was a happy little girl. I think when you have a child at an early age learn that they can *earn* what they want—that they don't just automatically *get* what they want—that they respect that. I think it makes them feel more independent, more mature. Raven learned early that she could *afford* her own doll without having to depend on someone else for it. That's powerful.

After we did that critical audition for *Ghost Dad*, and wound up getting the gig on *Cosby*, we went back to our one-bedroom apartment (we'd graduated from the horrible motel in Secaucus, but this new place had a few roaches, too!). We bought a massive bed for Raven because that's what she wanted with the money she'd earned. And the one bedroom was *her* room, and Lydia and I slept on the couch in the living room. We would have slept on the floor if we had to. Not that we were putting Raven on a pedestal. She'd simply earned that room through all her hard work and the great job she did.

The apartment was in Astoria, Queens, right around the corner from the studio where they filmed *Cosby*. With her money, we bought her an automatic, battery-operated Barbie car, and she actually drove that thing to work every day. She drove down the sidewalk, went through the studio doors, and straight into the elevator with that car, then down the hall, into her dressing room, beaming and proud. And justly so.

Get Real about a Good Work Ethic

Somehow Raven always knew the great importance of "the show." She was *aware* of how big it was, and how important her role was. Later, I found out the *Cosby* people had only planned to give her a few shows as Olivia Kendall. But her work ethic was so great (especially for a three-year-old) that they kept her on. She was always on time. She always gave 100 percent. She was always polite and respectful (of course, coming from the south, she was very "Yes, Ma'am, Yes, Sir," and still is). I sometimes carried stress and fear because that was *my child* out there after all, letting it all hang out. If she crumbles or gets hurt or even *destroyed*, I wouldn't have been able to live with myself. But she had fun, while at the same time, she always understood it was a job. That's a lot of responsibility for a small child. I mean, by that time, she couldn't just quit — "I'm takin' my ball and going home" — the way she could on the playground. Unfortunately, she couldn't even really get sick without big consequences for the whole production. Raven would have a horrible cold sore on Tuesday, the size of a toad, but somehow it would be gone by Friday, almost as though she could will it away in order to get the job done. The point is, she always delivered.

Now I'm not proposing that every toddler is ready for such responsibility, or wants such a big job to do. I am suggesting, though, that you can teach a healthy work ethic early. You can teach work-for-reward lessons early. You can share with your children your expectations, and you can hold them to those expectations. You can help them understand that there are consequences, good and bad, for their actions.

~

Get Real about Geographical Problems

It was difficult for Lydia and me to make the decision to move from Atlanta to New York to make Raven's dreams happen, but we had to do it. Location, sometimes, is everything. We knew Bill Cosby was the lynchpin to Raven's success, and we were unlikely to run into him in a shopping mall in Georgia. And this is one of the unavoidable facts of fulfilling your child's dream: You *might* have to uproot. You might need to be close to the city if that's where you need to be in order to find the right tutors or coaches, or the right school. You might need to be close to the country if the rodeo or, I don't know, snake-wrangling, is the dream. You might not need to move or to travel at all if your children's dreams don't call for it. That is fine, and this part of the equation is not a problem for you. You might be able to find everything you need in your own backyard.

But for some, especially those children who are interested in television, movies, stage acting, and so on, this move might, at some key point, need to happen. This story is as old as Hollywood or Broadway.

Although this is often one of the scariest things for parents to do, there are several reasons why this can be a great change for a family. A move gives a family the opportunity to grow closer together, strengthening bonds and widening horizons. **Without evolution, there's stagnation. Where there's change, there's life.** Because you often have your support system taken out from under you when you make a major move, you have to rely on your family for joy and encouragement. As poor as we were in those hovels in Jersey and New York, we had some of the best times of our lives together as a family.

Get Real about Rejection

Let's face it, your child won't succeed 100 percent of the time. Being realistic about your expectations means incorporating the idea of rejection. Once you have found a system that works for your family when dealing with your finances, health, geography, and especially communication, you are ready to define what success looks like.

When I first took Raven to New York, I was sure she was going to succeed, but that didn't stop some fears and doubts from creeping in sometimes. I had to get real about the possibility—the likelihood!—of some rejection. It was hard not to be disappointed after that receptionist at the William Morris Agency turned us away. It was hard when casting agents said she wasn't right for a part. But Raven wanted this more than anything, and her enthusiasm constantly reminded me that it's a numbers game. If, for every job you book, you've been rejected twenty times, then next time you know the math: Every rejection you get is just one move closer to that acceptance.

So we just had to set up little markers to reach. Getting auditions. Getting meetings. Learning lines. Booking small jobs. This made the whole process seem a lot less overwhelming. A year later, Raven was on *The Cosby Show*.

Get Real about School

Here are a few tips for helping your children cope with the woes of school, whether they're "A" students or "D" students. The goals here are to maximize the experience of school, considering it takes up most of their time and energy. Show your children that they should:

Focus on *learning*, not grades. It's the process of *how* your children think that matters more than what your children *know*, or even *what* they think. Once your children have a grasp on this they will be able to relax a bit more in school, and maybe even have a bit of fun learning.

Treat it like a game. It's not "cheating" to learn how to take tests well (consider the Princeton Review technique for "cracking the system" of the SATs and GREs). In the age of standardized testing and learning, it only makes sense to get a leg up on "the system."

Focus on what really matters to *them* among all the things they're learning that other people think are important. If they're interested in videogames, for example, they should try to see as much as they can through that lens: How is the study of a great work of literature like cracking the code to a videogame? What mathematical principles are behind the coding of their favorite game? What aspects of World War I would make a great videogame, and how would they set up the scenarios (the levels, the characters, and so on) to be historically accurate?

If your child has specific dreams, such as baking wedding cakes or acting, consider a specialty school such as a vocational school for culinary arts, or a performing arts school. Keep in mind, though, that these programs often require a base-level academic achievement.

Balance school with their other dreams, incorporating the two if possible. If their dream is to compete in the Boston Marathon at age fifteen, they're going to have to spend a lot of hours in training, at least as many as they do studying geometry.

Consider a *tutor* so they can focus on your specific dream. This can streamline an education, too. It might cost some money, but it will save your children potential time with potentially worse influences.

Remember there are a lot of important things in life besides school: What kind of person they are, their values, how they treat others, what they dream about, their talents, etc. Remind them not to compete against others. They should always strive for their *personal best.*

In the worst-case scenario, schools can kill dreams and potential. And even if the school experience isn't disastrous for your children, it can still function as a place of conformity and judgment, negativity and criticism. Of course you want to encourage your children to do as well as they can in school, but you don't want to get locked into acting like a deranged fanatic about something as unimportant in the big picture as the difference between a "B" and an "A." **School days can be painful and confusing for all children at one time or another, so help them learn to use this necessary time to shape their brains, to further their own goals, to learn *how to learn*, and to interact well with others.**

A MESSAGE FROM THE MEAN STREET KNOWN AS SESAME

Emily Perl Kingsley is a forty-year writer and producer for *Sesame Street*, winner of seventeen Emmys, author of twenty children's books, and parent of a special-needs son. She's also my good friend. Emily and I agree that the Dream Catcher principles can help your kid develop a good, meaningful dream that is *realizable* and in sync with that individual child's particular talents and abilities (and limitations), and then help them "go for it." But notice that little caveat within Emily's endorsement. She talks about "limitations," and I want to address that, using as many of Emily's own words as I can.

She hesitates to suggest that *all* dreams are achievable, however ambitious or unrealistic, even with energy, determination, and all the other right tools. "I'm afraid I just don't always think this is true," she says. "It would be a shame to set people up for this kind of journey and have them feel like 'failures' if they achieved anything short of the initial far-reaching dream." As Emily has in-depth experience dealing with special-needs children—her son has Down syndrome—it's worth hearing her out, even when my instincts tell me to shout, "But anything *is* possible!" It's important for us all to get real about certain legitimate limitations, as Emily experienced with her own son.

Emily tells the story of a particular little boy named "Matthew" who was a friend of her son, Jason. Matthew used to insist that he wanted to be president of the United States. He had been inculcated with the belief that he could achieve anything he put his mind to. In fact, that's just what his parents and counselors always told him. They meant well.

However, Emily offers a "reality check," despite her enormous optimism and belief in the power of children: There were inherent limitations, and reasons why Matthew would *never* become president, Emily says, no matter how sincerely he *wanted* it, how hard he tried, or how much his parents reinforced or encouraged him. Matthew had some severe physical and mental limitations. Emily's right. There was a lot that Matthew could have done with his life. But being president was definitely . . . well, some might say "impossible," but let's just say a "long shot."

Did he give up, though? Did he take a long, hard look at his limitations and decide he was good for nothing? *Not* by a long shot.

It took a while but Matthew has come to understand that there are wonderful, *achievable* goals that were "this side" of actually being president. To work for an elected official, to work for an organization that affects policy decisions, to participate on committees and boards of directors, to contribute to a better understanding of important issues by giving speeches and presentations, have become very satisfying and fulfilling career paths for Matthew.

Emily's point is that if Matthew had set his mind on becoming president *and nothing else would do* . . . he might have experienced some very discouraging and depressing periods in his life. And he might ultimately feel like a "failure."

So I think it's necessary here to take some advice from Emily, who knows much more about this kind of thing than I do, and express some latitude in my prescription for success. It's true that as parents we must take into account our children's individual abilities and limitations, as well as practical realities about the world and how it works, just in case the ultimate dream is not realized or realizable.

Emily advises parents that, "It has to be okay, ultimately, for a child to achieve a level of accomplishment that is gratifying and productive—even if it doesn't exactly correspond with the original dream." I agree with that. This is not to say don't shoot for the stars. But how many of us make it out of the atmosphere, no less to the moon? It's still a huge accomplishment. And we might not have ever gotten off the ground had we not *aimed high*.

A parent's job is not *only* to make a child's dream come true, Emily reminds us, but also to be a guide towards what is a realistic and achievable dream in the first place. "That is not to say we need to put our kids' dreams down . . . or limit them in the conceptualization phase . . . but to be there as an experienced adult who can intervene and counsel and guide kids when the world does not cooperate in making those original dreams come true."

At first blush, Emily's advice here might seem partly negative, or might seem to contradict my unbridled hopefulness—but it doesn't. Emily is "getting real" in the most sensible, healthy way possible, and I encourage you to do the same.

Winning Thinking

We've covered the practical issues, but we can't overlook getting real on an emotional level as well. I want to show you, so that you can show your children, about healthy and productive ways of thinking. Let me start with a story.

When I was nine, my family first moved to Atlanta from Bloomfield, Connecticut. My brother, Andre, who was four years older, used to listen to Motown, but I remember hearing the Stones's *Let It Bleed* album back then, too. I remember hearing their famous song, "You Can't Always Get What You Want." Now it seems to me there's some deep wisdom in the Stones's advice that if you're patient, you will always get what you *need*. By the early 1970s, a New York psychologist named Albert Ellis, founder of a behavior change system called Rational Emotive Behavior Therapy, or REBT, had gained national reputation for promoting the same powerful idea; the one that I adapted to help Raven on her journey.

Winning Thinking Through REBT

*R*ational   =   The way we think and reason

*E*motive   =   The way we feel

*B*ehavior   =   The way we act

*T*herapy   =   The way we heal ourselves and get better

The Winning Thinking method is a commonsense path to vastly improve the quality of your children's thinking, and therefore their lives. For millions, its predecessor, REBT, offered a kind of "miracle cure" for negative thinking, and for a select few, it offers a road to dream-fulfillment. After you learn a few basic principles, you can practice Winning Thinking on your own, at home, a little bit every day, and you can start showing your children right away how it works. Here are five techniques for Winning Thinking that I used with Raven, and use in my own life. See, the key to Winning Thinking is that it doesn't much matter what happens to you in life as long as you process it (think about it) in a healthy and productive way. The philosophy inherent in the lyrics to the song by the Stones is a perfect example of changing your thinking to adapt to reality, and finding yourself happier, more balanced, and more at peace as a result.

Only Thinking Makes It So

The most important lesson we can teach our children here is that it's *all in our heads*. We could radically change the world if we helped our children understand they alone are in charge of the processing plant in their head. They're the boss of that own factory of thoughts and feelings. Sure, raw "inputs" come into this factory all the time in the form of the things that happen around them (the stimuli or "Activating Events," as Ellis originally called them). But your children have a *choice* about how they process all these things that happen to them, and around them. They can choose how to order it, how to manipulate it, how to "make up their mind" about it, and perhaps most important, how to *respond* to it, how to act (the "output" of this factory), all according to what's in their head.

Now the truth is that most children already have some labor-relations and/or production problems with their thought factory. It can be a very unpleasant workplace. What matters is their *thoughts create their reality*, and that reality can be positive or negative, depending on those thoughts.

Let me be clear that the idea here is not to *blame* your children for their unhealthy thinking. I'm much more concerned with whether their thinking is likely to help them achieve what they want in life, or whether their thinking holds them back, or causes them suffering.

And of course I recognize that if your child has just become a paraplegic, heaven forbid, his bad feelings are in both his head *and* his legs. The important thing to teach that child is that only one of those things can be changed. He can't bring his legs back. But he can change what's in his head, so we should guide him to focus there, and only there.

You can allow your child to choose to feel victimized and worthless based on their situation—or you can help them train their brain to accept the reality of the circumstances, and move on toward a great life. Remember what Shakespeare's Hamlet says in Act II, Scene II: "There is nothing either good or bad, but thinking makes it so."

This brings me to the popular "Serenity Prayer," originally written by theologian Reinhold Niebuhr before World War II: "God, grant me the serenity to accept the things I cannot change; courage to change the things I can; and wisdom to know the difference." There's so much value in that statement. I wonder what we might achieve if we were to paint that phrase on every child's bedroom wall, and teach them how to read by it. At the least, we could model the sentiment in front of our children, and allow them to bask in our ability to move on from those things over which we have no control. The alternative is awful—our children will watch us bang our heads against the wall (our cruel boss, our empty bank account, our failed marriage). The core of the lesson is so simple, yet so hard for so many of us to comprehend: If you don't have any control of it, *stop* trying to control it! The only thing you can control is the way you think about things, including those things over which you have no control.

Most of you have probably heard of *The Secret*, the enormously popular book and movie by Rhonda Byrne. What is the Secret? It's that "every human being has the ability to transform any weakness or suffering into strength, perfect power, peace, health, and abundance." Sounds good, doesn't it? How do you do it, according to Byrne? You guessed it! By changing your thinking. It's true that a positive attitude and upbeat emotional state can change one's life for the better. And of course I believe that you can change your thinking to change your life.

But this basic precept of "positive thinking" is limited if you don't understand it correctly. In most cases, you can't bring your sight back once you've lost it, no matter how much you wish for sight. It's counterproductive to teach your children otherwise. In fact, you should teach them that they can't change their mean teacher (or the bully next door, or the other kid on the basketball court who keeps fouling people). **Instead, we can teach our children to** *deal with* **unpleasant things with a positive, peaceful outlook.** And we can't forget to teach them that they can change their *reply* to their cranky teacher, their *reaction* to the bully, and their *response* to the unsportsmanlike opponent. See the difference?

We are *response*-ible (required and able to respond) only for our part of these interactions. We're responsible for our thinking, which makes our reality so. According to Dr. Ellis, "you mainly feel the way you think." You mainly *feel the way you think*. There's another one for the bedroom wall. This means think like a winner, feel like a winner. Every time.

A Space to Choose

It would be extraordinary for their future if our children came to understand that it's not their evil teacher, their arch-nemesis down the block, that mean guard on the other side of the court (or even the seeming tragedy of a physical ailment, heaven forbid) that *makes* them feel bad. Between those factors and their responses to the factors, there lies a gap.

Try talking your children through this:

Mom has put a steaming apple pie on the windowsill and it "makes" you want to eat it, right? Or you thought you studied hard for that science test, but you got a "C," and that "makes" you angry and disappointed in yourself for being such a failure. That annoying kid on the bus makes a nasty comment about your *High School Musical* lunchbox, and it "causes" you to get embarrassed, and have a bad time all day at school. It seems like all these things are mere cause and effect, doesn't it? But is there another way to interpret these exchanges?

Sure there is. We should practice ourselves, then remind our children that we *choose* to respond to stimuli the way we do. How do we choose? A more accurate question is, *when* do we choose? This choosing happens in a short interval between stimulus and response, a "space to choose." In that space to choose, we can *deliberate, contemplate,* then *respond and act rationally and productively.*

What's on Your Mind?

The next step in training our children in Winning Thinking is to help them realize what usually happens in that space between what occurs around them and how they respond. It's all about what they *believe.* It's not too much homework, getting punished, being overweight, or anything else in the external world that makes your children feel the way they do. It's in what they think about the stimulus. *It's all in their head.* If their beliefs tell them they're a "failure" when they miss a pop fly, then they're going to be a failure. It's our responsibility to help our children overcome this challenge, by trying to get into that space to choose with them, and helping them make the best choices, the most healthy and productive way of thinking about the activating events. If, while we're in that space, we detect them thinking unproductively, we can do a quick correction. *You're not a "loser," you just missed the catch. Maybe we can practice some more after school, and you'll make the next one.* After a while, we can trust that they will be able to process things properly in their thought-factory; they can be their own thought-foreman.

Talk Ain't Cheap

Along with what we believe comes what we say to ourselves in that space to choose. So often, what we say is poisonous. So a key step in teaching Winning Thinking is to understand that many of life's challenges can be overcome by not focusing on our feelings and emotions (the outcome) so much as focusing on the messages we give ourselves—the "self-talk" connected to our beliefs—that so often fuels those feelings and emotions. Our children need to replace their "Blocking Beliefs" with "Rockin' Beliefs." See in the examples below how our beliefs go hand-in-hand with our self-talk, and lead to negative consequences like emotional upset.

Blocking Beliefs or Rockin' Beliefs?
Unhealthy, Irrational, Counterproductive Beliefs and Self-Talk Versus Healthy, Rational, Productive Beliefs and Self-Talk

BLOCKING	ROCKIN'
"They didn't pick me for the team. I'm such a loser."	"I guess I'm not the best volleyball player. I'm going to practice my serves this weekend with my friends."
"Why I am I so afraid to ask him out on a date? I'm such a wimp!"	"You know, this summer I biked twenty miles in one day! I can do just about anything if I decide to do it. And I'm going to ask him out!"
"The teacher makes me feel stupid with all that complicated stuff about the Revolutionary War. I'll never get ahead in this class."	"I don't understand what the teacher has been teaching lately. I'd better ask some questions so I understand better, and maybe ask my parents for some extra help. I want to learn as much as I can about history, because I really want to get it."
"So, I'm the fattest girl in class now. What a pig! Guess it's just a matter of time now before they start calling me 'The Whale.'"	"I don't like the idea that I've gained weight. It would be good for me to learn as much as I can about how to eat healthier and get in shape—I care about myself, so I want to take care of myself. You know, this is a helpful wakeup call."
"Well, I didn't finish mowing the lawn, so I might as well not set the table either, since Mom will be mad at me anyway."	"It wasn't cool of me to not finish the lawn. I'm going to set the table, apologize to Mom, and make sure I do all my chores tomorrow."

~

Love Your *Self*

It's one of those painfully obvious principles that can nevertheless be somewhat hard to put into practice. But once you have mastered it in your own life, you can model this for your children, and show them how to use it. The philosophy has origins back in REBT, where it's called "Unconditional Self-Acceptance": The rules are simple: Stop judging yourself. I mean stop judging your *self*. This means you can always criticize your behaviors and your decisions, and you can make necessary changes accordingly. If we work hard, don't cheat, and eat a nice balanced meal, we think of our *selves* as good. *I'm a good person.* But if we steal an apple from the grocer, or eat a whole carton of ice cream, or lie to our principal, we think of our *selves* as fundamentally bad.

But you're not a bad *person* because you set yourself a goal of practicing your oboe for an hour, and you only made it for half an hour. You have just *behaved* in a way that did not further your goal of becoming a world-class oboe player as much as it could have had you spent more time.

Unfortunately, loving your self does not come easy, especially after a lifetime of negative self-talk. You have to keep working on it, every day, for the rest of your life. That sounds depressing, but actually, you can experience the benefits of Winning Thinking immediately if you give it a shot. Each time you do, it gets easier.

Think of it as "mental fitness." It will get easier as you get mentally fitter, but if you stop practicing, you'll get flabby again, and probably resort to that old stinkin' thinkin'. Remember, if your children struggle with any of these principles at first, don't let them get down on themselves for it—"I'm so stupid I can't even accept myself unconditionally." Obviously, that would miss the point entirely!

Spot Blocking Beliefs

Now, while you're in that space to choose with your children, between something that happens to them, and their response, you should be conscious of what they are saying to themselves, what "self-talk scripts" (beliefs) come up. I say "scripts," because often, children repeat self-defeating talk, which continually reinforces unhealthy beliefs and perpetuates bad feelings: Let's say they fell off the balance beam during a local gymnastics competition, and the coach yelled at them in front of all their friends. Now whenever your child thinks about that scene, they replay those feelings, tell themselves the same thing, and do still more unproductive thinking, like, "My coach was right. I am a klutz," or "I'll never make the Regionals. It started when I missed that beam, and now it's hopeless. Gymnastics is just humiliating!"

You should teach your children that not all thoughts are equally valuable. In fact, some thoughts are "rational," and some are "irrational." Irrational thoughts and feelings are simply those that block you from achieving your goals. They fuel extreme emotions like rage, stinging humiliation, bitter disappointment, and hopelessness. Irrational beliefs also tend to distort reality—they contain exaggerated or otherwise illogical ways of evaluating oneself, others, and the world. In the following Irrational Beliefs and Toxic Self-Talk scripts, look for exaggerations and distortions, and look for what we call "demandments" (extreme and impossible demands we place on ourselves, others, and the world):

- "He *can't* give us this much homework every night. He *has* to give us less!"
- "I *must* always train for five hours every day or I'll *never* be a great bowler."
- "She *should* do the same amount of chores as I."
- "It's *not fair* that he gets to eat more dessert!"
- "I *never* get to do the stuff I want to do."
- "When I train for cross-country, the pain in my legs is just *awful!* The *worst!* I *can't stand it!*" (Therapists call this one "awfulizing," or, less artfully, "catastrophizing.")

You can see how frustrating it would be for your children to live in this kind of world, where they constantly demand the world work a certain way—and it never does. The secret is to get real. It's probably not really *that bad*. It's not that you *never* get what you want. It's not that he *must* do things a certain way. *Must?* According to whom?

Replace with Rockin' Beliefs

You can help your children realize that they can replace their usual Blocking Beliefs and Poisonous Self-Talk with more rational, healthy ways of believing, thinking, and talking to themselves—"Rockin' Beliefs." They can learn to dispute and replace Blocking Beliefs to do this. Here are a few good ways:

Model Winning Thinking, and teach your children to be rational, to really think it out, to "get real." Teach them that there's no law that says anything really *must* be a certain way. Is it bad that Mommy and Daddy got a divorce? Maybe. But can one rationally argue that there's some law of the Universe that one's parents absolutely ought not to get divorced? This is mental fitness, so you have to do it for yourself every day until you get good enough to teach it to your children. Eventually, it will gain a foothold in your subconscious, and your children's. Then look out, world!

Show your children how to use a "disaster scale" to put things in perspective. Imagine that a 1 on this scale is not bad at all, really quite tolerable, and a 10 is the worst thing that ever happened, literally deadly. When you hear your children saying (or you suspect they're thinking), "I *can't stand* this summer camp anymore. This is the *absolute worst* place on Earth. It's *unbearable*," hear them out, then show them how to slow down, breathe, sit a while allowing them to feel safe, and get real (think rationally):

Can they stand it? Yes—they can. They're standing it right now. They could probably stand a whole lot worse if they had to.

Is it the absolute worst thing that could ever happen? No— there are far worse things that could happen, and even those could still be worse into infinity. Realize that whatever they're going through is very often *not that bad*. It might be just that they keep telling themselves it's bad. Or it might just be *unpleasant*, but it's probably *not unendurable*.

Is it unbearable? Come on! Look what our parents endured. Look what their parents endured. There have been millions of people who put things in perspective to keep hope alive in very dire circumstances far worse than missing their favorite TV show in order to study lines. Viktor Frankl's *Man's Search for Meaning* comes to mind. Hope in the Holocaust? It's possible. It's what saved Frankl, even after he saw his family slaughtered.

Help your children to replace overgeneralizations, magnifications, and all-or-nothing thinking, as these are irrational—they don't get us where we want to go. They don't "always" miss the basket. They don't have the "world's biggest nose." They haven't "blown their chances of an 'A' completely" if they bomb one test—as long as they don't keep bombing.

Please don't ever forget that thinking, whether your beliefs are "Blocking" or "Rockin'," is self-perpetuating and self-fulfilling. "The mind moves in the direction of our currently dominant thoughts," said Earl Nightingale: "You become what you think about."

Welcome to the Real World

More often than not, parents view obstacles as tremendous roadblocks rather than mere limiting steps. But the vast majority of such obstacles can be overcome. I encourage you to "get real" without "getting down." Sure, be aware of the "real world," but also be aware of the awesome power of the human will, and the power of the Source to make things happen. Achieving a dream might seem unattainable when your idea of the "real world" is clouded by ideas like "impossible" and "never."

Or how about Jason Kingsley, Emily's son? He became an award-winning author.

Dreams really can come true.

We have the power and the strength and the fortitude to triumph over unbelievable odds, to achieve the impossible, as Jason proves.

This Dream Catcher doesn't filter out reality, but reminds us we just have to *get real* about the steps we have to take— we have to know it won't be easy, it won't happen overnight, and it won't happen without a few bumps and scratches at the least.

Dream Catcher Six

Kill Fear

I have learned over the years that when one's mind is made up, this diminishes fear; knowing what must be done does away with fear.

—Rosa Parks, civil rights activist

Fear is a dream killer. A great fear among parents is that their child will feel bad when life is hard. I chose not to give in to fear, and prepared my daughter to feel good about herself even when the going got tough. While it's natural and healthy to fear for your child, if you allow your *own fears and insecurities* to stymie the enormous potential you have to foster your child's dreams, to influence their self-esteem, their happiness, and the practical facts of their future, you'll doom the both of you. But we'll see in this Dream Catcher that that doesn't have to happen! Here, you'll find a plan that will help you overcome your own fears, and show you how to help your children overcome their fears—especially their fear of so-called failure.

Free Yourself from Fear!

A friend of mine from L.A. recently confided that when she goes into the bathroom for a shower, she makes her eleven-year-old kid hide out in his bedroom. She's just absolutely terrified that something awful will happen to her child when she's not literally watching. It's not like she's living in a crime-riddled neighborhood, either. Of course I'm all for protecting our children, and looking out for them whenever we can, but there is such a thing as overprotection. This mother, though loving and well-meaning, will inevitably implant in her child her worst fears. She's cultivating a kid who's learning to panic about the world, rather than learning to embrace it. Not to mention, she herself is seriously stressed because of all the fear!

When I reminisce about my own mother, I realize she wasn't perfect, of course, but I'm so grateful she didn't unconsciously victimize me like that. She gave me the free-dom to grow. She didn't pass on her own apprehensions. She trusted me, and I guess she trusted the neighborhood, knowing there were "eyes" all around. When I think about it, it seems like parents in general were more trusting back in the day. Sure, bad things sometimes happened back then, even to kids, but parents didn't *assume* something terrible would happen to their kids if they were alone for a couple of hours.

To be honest, when I was a little kid in Connecticut, we kids were alone for a lot more than just a couple of hours. My mother and the other mothers on the block used to tell us to "go play in the woods," and that's exactly what we did.

Sometimes from dawn till dusk. We had fun, independently, and we grew, organically. We learned about ourselves and each other, and we learned to embrace new things—strange bugs, animals, caves, etc.—rather than fear them. I don't think that ever would have happened had my mother been a worry-wart. She knew that she'd taught me well, instilled the right values, guided me to make good judgments in the face of all those inevitable choices.

My mother was all about easing fear. I remember when I was very little, if I got a mosquito bite, I'd come to her whining, looking for comfort, really looking for her to sympathize. She'd gently trace an "X" over the bite with her fingernail, kiss it, and assure me it was okay. As I've said before, you do the best you can as a parent, given the tools you bring to the table. My mother didn't have a PhD in early childhood development, but she somehow intuitively understood that we bring all our beliefs into our parenting, and we pass them on to our children, often unwittingly, often in direct opposition to what we're trying to impart. My mom got this one right: *There's nothing to worry about, Kiddo*. Quit crying. It's just a tiny bug bite.

I try hard not to judge other parents when I witness them interacting with their kids, but when it comes to them passing on their own fears, I want to tell them that they should seriously consider throwing all their beliefs away, and starting from scratch, searching inside the deep well of themselves, and knowing, as my mom did, *It's going to be all right*. It's been all right for a very, very long time, you know. Up and down, sure, and sometimes pretty far down, for some people. But in the big picture, it's going to be all right.

It's so hard to truly realize that as a parent—especially as a new parent. Every moment seems to provide a new opportunity to fear something. *He's going to fall down and break his neck. She'll smash her face on that glass door. He'll talk to strangers. She won't look both ways. He'll touch the stove. He's setting himself up for a huge disappointment.* And of course it's natural to worry. It's your job to look after your children. You asked for it—you got it. What I'm talking about is not *imposing* your own fears, your own limitations, on a child when it's your responsibility instead to nurture his success.

When I was five, one of the greatest science fiction books in history came out. Frank Herbert's *Dune* was at the height of its popularity when I was a teenager. In it, a mother teaches her son, Paul, this litany, to keep him from fear in times of peril: "I must not fear. Fear is the mind-killer. Fear is the little-death that brings total obliteration. I will face my fear. I will permit it to pass over me and through me. And when it has gone past I will turn the inner eye to see its path. Where the fear has gone there will be nothing. Only I will remain."

Awesome. You don't have to be a sci-fi geek for that philosophy to resonate. And you don't have to be some kind of Jedi to master the technique. It's merely about mind over matter. Or, actually, it's all about mind over what-seems-like-matter-but-that's-only-in-your-mind.

Fear is a form of psychological infection. Some call it "the paralysis of analysis." David J. Schwartz talks about this in his book *The Magic of Thinking Big.* He says "We can cure a mental infection the same way we cure a body infection—with specific, proved treatments . . . *action cures fear.* Indecision, postponement, on the other hand, fertilize fear. . . . Jot that down in your success rule book right now. Action cures fear."

You see, you don't have to perform all kinds of mental gymnastics to overcome a fear: You need only to act. Move forward. Face it. Do it. The mental state will follow the action.

Fear Is in the "Little You"

In the third grade I was in the chorus. I guess I had gotten good enough, because by the end of the year, I was scheduled for a solo at a big performance, in front of an auditorium packed with people. This solo stays in my mind for a few reasons I want to share, in the hope that it will be useful for parents working on helping their children overcome their fears. Many of you will relate when I say when it came time to do the solo, it was pretty easy, and I was in the moment. But waiting for it, planning for it, imagining all the things that could go wrong, was debilitating. I became almost crippled. Psychologists call this "anticipatory anxiety," and it's very often worse than actual performance anxiety. It definitely was for me. When I thought about it—my teacher counting on me, my friends all watching, my parents dressed up and waiting to be proud—my heart literally skipped beats. I sweated. My mouth got dry. Even now, forty years later, when I think back, those feelings are still lurking somewhere in that primal, fearful place inside us all. The moment right before stepping out on stage, right in the spotlight, was the worst. But I started my solo.

At first, the fear squeezed my voice so much it actually changed the tonality, and I wound up singing at such a high range. It must have been comical. But not to me. I was disappointed in myself, because it wasn't coming out as I'd practiced, as I'd hoped. I still remember the pain of those first few seconds. But the fear somehow didn't cause me to simply shut down and run away. I stuck it out. *I took the action that cured the fear.* I didn't want to be the kind of kid who spent his whole life trembling in the wings, worried about the upcoming performance. I knew kids like that. It seemed to me it must be what hell is like. Some voice was saying to me, "Dude, you're out here. Just sing." If you're truly singing, really in the moment, there's no space in you for fear.

Everyone said my performance was beautiful. I took a powerful lesson from this as I looked back in retrospect when I had a daughter afraid to step into that spotlight and sing. What we have to do when faced with such fear, is twofold. One, like the Nike ad, is *just do it*. Do it now! It's scary on the diving platform, looking down at the water below. But once you go, you can't help but laugh. It's fun. And two, if you just can't seem to make the leap, go deep inside yourself for a moment, and find that place where there's *a knowing*. That place that knows you can do it, and you'll be okay.

Help Your Children Face Their Fears

Raven had this one fear that kept recurring. When little fears—and occasionally big ones—crept into her consciousness, I had to remind her that she had nothing to fear. I mean literally nothing. I reminded her she'd learned every script so far. She gave her A-game at every photo shoot. She performed to perfection in front of thousands. She made Bill Cosby laugh! But she was afraid of singing the national anthem at professional ball games. Even though she practiced and practiced, drilled and drilled, even with singing coaches and lots of experience, the thought of those first notes, the "*Ohhh-ohhh say . . .*" of our anthem always scared her. But action cures fear. You'll stand there shivering forever—or you'll get over it as soon as you sing that first note. You face your fear head on, and you get through it. You conquer not by retreating, but by advancing. It's the same on roller coasters, isn't it? It's scary ratcheting up and up, but once you start to whoosh down, it's all good. At the end of the anthem, Raven got the applause and the thrill that comes with knowing that she'd done it. She'd faced it. She killed it. And the next time was that much easier.

You can help your children overcome their fears the same way. If Sasha is afraid of the batter's box, just get her in there. Let her get the experience of knocking a few out of the park—and of swinging and missing, too. Either way, next time will be more manageable. Our greatest fears seem to stem from the unknown. Once the batter's box becomes home, she might still experience a little normal performance anxiety (in fact a little stress in this situation can actually improve performance, scientists say)—but at least she won't be paralyzed with fear.

Quelling Your Own Fears

If you ever watch Cesar Millan's *Dog Whisperer*, you'll know what he says about fear: Dogs can sense it on you. And if you approach them with fear, you're going to get bitten. If, on the other hand, you come to the dog with a calm, confident, and dominant energy, the dog will submit. The world is like that dog. If you're afraid you're going to get bitten, better get ready for that bite.

But what about the fears that *we* feel for our children? The biggest thing we're afraid of is that our children will experience rejection and disappointment. But is that rational? Eventually, they're going to have to deal with those inevitabilities. Countless other parents overcame this fear, and helped their children achieve their dreams. Deborah Phelps, who fought teachers and other naysayers to raise her son Michael to believe in his dream of becoming a world-class swimmer. Michael Phelps broke crazy records. "Big Russ" Russert, a garbage man in Buffalo, New York, whose dream was that his son Tim would go to college and become a lawyer. Tim went on to become the host of *Meet the Press*, and one of the leading TV political analysts in the country. Star New York Giants running back Tiki Barber's mother, Geraldine, ignored doctors and coaches who told her that her son should never play contact sports because he was too small and weak! Amazon .com's Jeff Bezos had parents who invested the $300,000 they had saved for retirement in their son's fledgling online venture. And we know how that turned out!

These parents wouldn't succumb to fear of rejection and disappointment. They put it all out there, believing strongly that their children would succeed. In some ways, like me, they refused to let fear take a front seat. Sure, worries were always there in the back seat, but they and their children were in the driver's seat!

I know countless other parents, less well-known, but no less heroic, who helped their children achieve their dreams. My friends Rebecca and David, who had been told that their dyslexic daughter, Julia, should be content with low grades in school and an "easy" career that didn't involve much reading or writing. But Julia wanted more than anything to be a doctor. Rebecca and David told her that was absolutely achievable. They fought the school system to get Julia the extra tutoring she needed, researched technology that made it easier for her to read her textbooks, and most important, they defeated their own fears of Julia "failing," and they helped her overcome her own fears, too. Julia is a pediatrician now, and she helps other children triumph over their fears.

"The Only Thing We Have To Fear," FDR's first inaugural speech in 1932, said it all. It is perhaps the most valuable thing ever said about fear: "The only thing we have to fear is fear itself—nameless, unreasoning, unjustified terror which paralyzes needed efforts to convert retreat into advance."

~

Don't Fear the Bear

I've already demonstrated that action cures fear. But this principle works in the opposite direction, too. Certain actions *cause* fear. Consider the case of running from a bear, according to the American philosopher and psychologist, William James, who wrote "What Is an Emotion?" for a magazine called *Mind* in 1884. It's not that we see a bear, are afraid, and run away. It's that we see a bear, run away, and *there-fore* are afraid. But what's behind that "*therefore?*" Basically, the idea is simple. James believed, as I do, that emotions—like fear and joy—come along with physical responses in the body (such as a thumping heart, sweaty palms, a balled-up stomach, etc.).

We see a bear. Our muscles tense up, our nerves get jangly, and our heart skips a beat. These things all happen in our sympathetic nervous system, in "sympathy" with our emotions, and they all create a sense of "reality": It *feels* scary, and that fear feels very real. But you can see it's not the bear causing the "reality" of fear. Instead, the fear starts inward and manifests outward. Neuroscientists argue that our emotions *feel* different from other states of mind (like concentration, reasoning, or some kinds of memory) because they are so associated with these bodily responses. The responses, almost by definition, occasion internal sensations. Sadness feels different from joy, and fear from confidence, because of their different bodily responses and sensations.

So, we see a bear, says James, and we turn tail and run. While we flee, the body goes through a physiological upheaval: Our blood pressure and our heart rate go up, our pupils dilate, our palms sweat, and our muscles contract. We might even s**t our pants, because this, too, is a natural, physiological response, an innate defense mechanism left over from our caveman days when we needed to lighten the load as we fled.

Notice that if we see a beautiful butterfly, our body will go through different physiological commotions. But either way, the physical changes in the body travel back to the brain where the brain "senses" them in a kind of "sensory feedback loop," with each emotion having its own unique physiological sense signature. What's the lesson here? Change the physical state, and change the emotion. Change the messages you send to your brain, change your brain, where the emotion is recognized. Interrupt the feedback loop. Show your children: When you're halfway up the basement stairs, and the hairs on the back of your neck stand up for fear of what's behind you, stop. Turn around. Boldly and confidently face them down. Tell yourself, "I am fearless." Change your body posture (don't slump or slink, but stand up straight). In short, when you "Act As If" you're not afraid (see "Dream Catcher Two: Believe It")—you literally won't be afraid.

Motivational speaker Anthony Robbins puts an extra twist on this. Because, as James posited, an emotion (such as fear) is only the mind's *perception of the physical state* (the racing heart and the high adrenaline); you can short-circuit the emotion by radically interrupting the perception. So if someone is weeping (seemingly uncontrollably), Robbins will get right in their face and yell at them violently, something like, "Stop crying now!" The person is so shocked that they typically immediately stop crying. He's proven that people are effectively *choosing* to continue to feel the way they're feeling. We know this emotion-interrupter works because we do it all the time to calm crying children. Carrying them wailing, what do we do? We take them to the window and show them the horses. Or we shake our keys at them, or put some shiny bauble in their field of vision. We know that they're *deciding* to throw a tantrum, and they could just as easily decide on something else, if we can distract them long enough to make a different decision.

Identifying the Top Three Types of Fear

If you want your children to succeed, not only in fulfilling their dreams, but also in feeling balanced and confident on a day-to-day basis, it helps to give them tools to conquer their fears. Anyone who's suffered the grip of crippling fear knows what a relief would come with strangling that enemy, killing the fear, and stepping out into the freedom to move on boldly in pursuit of their dreams. But what weapon do you use to kill fear? What's the Kryptonite for fear? We better find it fast or it will snap at our ankles, hamstring our goals, and smother our dreams. But in order to slay fear, we have to understand its several incarnations. This monster comes in three main forms, and each form requires different kinds of poison to die:

1. Rational fear. These fears kick in when we go into survival mode, because they tend to work on a primal, instinctual level. If little Tommy is thrown into a pit of vipers, for example, he probably *ought* to be afraid.

2. Irrational Fear. The second kind of fear is more subtle, and will probably *not* save Tommy from certain death by snakebite, but can actually poison him from the inside. Despite Tommy's long practicing, he breaks into a cold sweat at the thought of missing his first foul shot. The noise of the crowds, the tension between the team and the coach, Tommy's friends in the stands—all these factors contribute to the fear rising from deep inside him. We'd label this fear as "irrational" because it has no basis in fact (no shiny fangs and rattling tail).

3. Anxiety. These are even more subtle than Tommy's basketball court scenario. Here, we don't even have a big game to fear. Anxieties are more free-floating and amorphous—it's hard to tie them to any specific circumstance or situation in our lives, like a big game. Neurotic anxiety means that Little Tommy suffers a constant *feeling* that things are all wrong, that he's not in control, the world is somehow against him.

Slaying the Dragons of Fear

Now that we've identified the three main types of fear, you can discern which of your children's fears fall into each category: which are "irrational" and which "rational." Hint: The vast majority will be irrational. No parent would advise a child to face her fear of a hungry shark by jumping in with the chum—that fear is totally rational. So we're going to deal here with the second type of fear. We're going to focus on the last two, irrational fears and anxiety, because those are the two over which we can teach our children to have the most control.

Fear might *feel* unconquerable, but several straightforward principles that I used with Raven to defeat fear and focus on her dreams can help you and your children, too.

Decide which of the two irrational fears your child is feeling. (Again, if their fear is rational, you have a bigger problem than helping them overcome their fear—you have to get them out of the shark tank!) Is the fear tied to a specific event, person, class, subject, performance, or other aspect of their lives—or is it free-floating? If it's the former, you can use the Dream Catchers in this book to help alleviate the fear (with belief, positive visualization, drilling, self-affirmation, relaxation methods, etc.). If it's the latter, you can work on an overall plan for reducing anxiety (see the section on meditation in "Dream Catcher Four: Aim Straight").

Help your children trace the fear back to its origin. What specifically scares them about getting on stage? Is it the people watching? Is it their peers making fun of them? Is it their potential inadequacy contrasted to the other actors? What about camping at night makes them anxious? Fear of the dark? Scary animals? Of being far from home? This natural progression of questions helps your children understand where the fear comes from, so that, together, you can face it, and start talking through solutions. Chances are a little baby fear monster was hatched inside them, and after it was fed and nurtured, it grew into something bigger and more debilitating. This monster thrives in the dark, so once it's dragged out into the light, it will suffer and die.

Remember that worry solves nothing. Our worries nourish the monster we are trying to kill by giving it bites of our time and our energy—time and energy that should be focused positively, constructively, proactively. It's okay to think about problems and solutions. It's okay to review mistakes and to plan for contingencies. But hours of brooding and worrying about things over which they have no control is like giving free rent in their consciousness to a mean monster that lives upstairs. Evict him! Banish him from the premises. As Jesus says in his Sermon on the Mount, "Therefore do not be anxious about tomorrow, for tomorrow will be anxious for itself" (Matthew 6:34).

Counteract the fear by focusing on the positives. If Amy loves to play music in her band but chokes every time she gets on stage to perform, talk to her about what she loves about playing music with people. Ask her, "What's your favorite part about playing in your band? Is it hanging out with your friends in the band? Is it seeing the fans connect with the message of your songs? Is it just rockin' out?" The positives will remind Amy why she chose to pursue her dream in the first place; redirect her attention away from her fears and back to her passion for her musical dream.

Use the techniques in "Dream Catcher Three: Picture It" to work with your children on visualizing themselves in the future, having slain their fear dragon, having conquered the fear that now plagues them. Be creative with this exercise, and remember to make the vision vivid and emotional: Maybe your child's fear is some leviathan he's harpooning; or perhaps it's King Kong that he's shooting off his tower.

When images or feelings of fear reappear, show your children how to recognize them, confront them, and challenge them. Encourage your children to internally dialogue with the negativity. "Hey, I'm not afraid of you!"

In the end, I include killing fear as an important Dream Catcher because fear is the natural enemy of dreams. **We need to help our children filter out irrational fears in order to free their minds to pursue their dreams.** The late Bonaro W. Overstreet, an author, poet, and psychologist, summed it up well. She wrote, "Perhaps the most important thing we can undertake toward the reduction of fear is to make it easier for people to accept themselves, to like themselves." Overstreet's idea is a profound one. Fear and self-doubt, self-recrimination, are the same kind of monster, and both must be killed before we move on. Fear is too heavy to carry on the road to your dreams.

Dream Catcher Seven

Do Good

Do all the good you can, by all the means you can, in all the ways you can, in all the places you can, at all the times you can, to all the people you can, as long as ever you can.

—John Wesley, eighteenth-century Anglican cleric

It's time to open a dialogue about values and how to prioritize them for balance and good mental health. For example, you wouldn't want to encourage your children to be mean or to harm others on the way to their dreams. Here, we'll discuss the values that will not only help you raise successful children, but help you raise *good* children, too. Foremost among these, ensuring that your child is aware, empathetic, and respectful of others, is a necessary step on the journey. This Dream Catcher reminds us of the time-honored principle: If you do good, you get good things back.

The Great Circle

It seems to me that life, if lived in accordance with nature, is about reciprocity. You can show this to even your smallest children. For example, the elm tree in your back yard breathes out oxygen so you may breathe it in. In turn, you breathe out carbon dioxide, which the tree takes in to sustain its life. This is how the Universe works. The flower gives its nectar to the bumblebee, and in turn, the bee gives the flower the gift of pollination. The clouds give rain to all of us living creatures, and the seeds give us nourishment. But in the modern world most of us have lost touch with this fundamental principle of life, so we've stopped trying to operate the way nature operates. We work as though we're all separate, as though symbiosis doesn't matter. Or if we do understand the concept of give-and-take, we focus mostly on the "take" part, always scheming about what we can get out of others and the world.

Although this strategy might satisfy for a while, such a self-serving philosophy will ultimately, invariably, cause a person great pain and frustration. The horticultural metaphor is useful here: Notice I didn't describe the bee as *taking* the nectar, but rather the flower as *giving* the nectar, offering its bounty willingly, by design. In fact, its very survival depends on that willingness to give of itself. Instead of concentrating on what it can gain from the bee, it puts its energy (literally) into providing something desirable, beneficial, and useful for the bee. The Universe working the way it does, the flower of course *does* gain, by this law of reciprocity. The bee helps spread the seed so the flower can propagate and thrive.

You can show the same essential generosity in your own life, and reap enormous rewards in the end. So the question you need to ask your children is, *What's your nectar?* What special element do you have that you can give away to the planet, unselfishly, to make the world a better place? If you can find that nectar and give it away, a Source will give you back in spades, and you, like the flower, will propagate and thrive.

Of course, as parents, you already understand this idea. Why do you give so unselfishly to your children? Your time, your love, your food, and everything else? Do you give because you expect to get something back? No. You give because that's the law of the Universe. But naturally you *do* get something back. I'm not talking about pride, or satisfaction, or even someone to take care of you when you get old and frail. You get back something far greater: You get the continuance of your species. You get life itself, way into the future beyond your reckoning. That seems like a pretty good deal, even given how frustrating it sometimes is to be a parent.

The Green Stuff

So what do we teach our children to give? If you're blessed the way Raven is, maybe you can give away money. Of all the cool stuff my daughter has achieved, one of the things I'm most proud of is her philanthropic work. Because diabetes runs in her mother's family, Raven has been particularly generous with the Juvenile Diabetes Foundation, but she's donated to many causes, including the Red Cross, the

Women's Alive Coalition, and the Children's Miracle Network. Raven's made an empire for Disney worth nearly half a billion dollars, but it's what she's given back that matters more to me as a proud father. I will suggest here that when you discuss with your child the "value" of money, to include in that discussion the idea of *relative wealth*: There are always those who are poorer, and more in need, and sometimes money can help make their lives better. You can introduce this seemingly adult concept in the context of "sharing," which even the smallest children can grasp.

Along those lines, I want to briefly share a little trick about money that complies with the law of reciprocity. If you think about the money as an end unto itself, it won't come as quickly—if at all—as it will if you think about what you can *give* (instead of what you can get in return). In my experience, people who think of their jobs as opportunities to give something away to others (a beautiful voice, a desire to serve and protect, a passion to teach, or some other special skill) almost always make more money than people who think of their jobs as a mere means to a financial end.

And once that money comes in, those who responsibly give back through charity and philanthropy, tend to find that some Source of all things gives back to them in ways they didn't plan for. Sometimes the Universe gives back money, in the form of new opportunities and windfalls, and sometimes it reciprocates with a powerful feeling that you just can't buy. But it always gives back. *Always*.

So how do you teach this to your children? Well, first, as usual, you can model it. Show your children some sensible and conscientious charity where it's most needed, and explain why you're doing it: "You know how our beagle Jupiter has a warm bed and lots of love and snacks? Well, not every dog has those great things. Some dogs are cold and lonely and even hungry. But we can help. We work hard and we make enough money to give some of it away to help those poor dogs. Don't you think we should do that? What about if it means maybe we can only afford to buy you one toy this weekend instead of two?"

Whatever your attitudes toward money, another concept worth teaching your child is the idea that material stuff doesn't matter as much as the intangibles in life. *You can't take it with you.* Not to get your children thinking about death, but thinking about what really matters, what really has value. Love. Family. Health. Security. Pride. A good name. You have your own list. Share it. Discuss it. Impart it.

———— IF YOU WANT TO BE HAPPY FOR THE ————
REST OF YOUR LIFE. . . .

Arthur C. Brooks wrote an interesting book about this subject, *Gross National Happiness*. In it he argues that the best way to be happy is to *give money away*. People who support charitable causes (and people who volunteer their time) are nearly twice as likely as non-givers to report that they're very happy.

Other Gifts

My parents provided a crystal-clear example of giving, on an almost daily basis. My father served his country with pride and honor, and was so dedicated he was often gone for many months—sometimes years—at a time (while he served in Korea). And my mother served her students, giving the best of herself every day.

This spirit of giving seemed to have rubbed off on Raven. While I think that she was naturally giving, Lydia and I and all her grandparents reinforced in her that if one is blessed in life, one should try to bless others. Even before she had big money to give away, Raven was able to use an even more powerful gift to bring millions of people joy and happiness: her humor. I can't tell you how many people I've met whose eyes light up when they talk about Raven-Symoné. In turn, giving away that gift has brought back to Raven a joyous and rewarding life. This is good to remember when it seems like money is too tight to allow for any charitable giving.

In fact it might be even more of a blessing to give of yourself in some non-financial way. Perhaps you can give your time. Your expertise. Your public service. As a director and producer, it's a great feeling to have given many people jobs and opportunities and a good living. In end credits after movies or TV shows, and in the liner notes on albums, I sometimes see the familiar names of people I helped "bring up," people who got their first break from me. They did me a huge service by helping me, and now I can see that the Universe has rewarded them. I'm thinking of one guy in particular here: Courtney Miller. He was maybe eighteen when Raven was nine and in need of a choreographer. Later he did choreography for *That's So Raven* and *The Cheetah Girls*—not to mention for Michael Jackson!

Along the way, we did a lot of stuff for no fee. When people needed things, we tried to give wherever we could, and Raven still does. I don't think it was ever to our detriment. We did some fun and crazy Public Service Announcements for NBC-TV. This was when "The More You Know" campaign first started. Raven and I did one on paternal involvement.

We tried to help Raven understand that in the public eye, she was blessed to achieve a certain stature, and it was her responsibility to highlight the good about herself, her family, and her people. She liked the idea of helping the world in some small way, helping to make it better. I think most children have that gene in them somewhere.

Random Acts of Kindness: How Do We Pay It Forward?

Let's admit it: We want people to do good things for us, to do right by us. This principle is so important and fundamental that they call it the "Golden Rule." You can help children understand this by asking them, "You wouldn't like it very much if someone deliberately tripped you while you were walking down the street, would you?" But what if you were walking down the street and someone gave you a warm "Hello" and a present? Surely that would be a more pleasant experience.

Yet, it seems that in the hustle and bustle of everyday life, we often end up serving only ourselves, or those immediately around us, with little regard for those who might be out there in need of that "Hello," or that gift, whatever we can afford. See, the best way to create the kind of world where people get warm "Hellos" and great presents is not to sit around waiting to receive that sort of stuff, but to give it. Be the kind of person who gives others a warm "Hello" and a gift of yourself. This is a surefire way to feel better about the Universe.

Sometimes we need to forfeit the good we want for ourselves (or our family) for the sake of those who need that little something. It's not really a forfeit. We can start showing our children this—not to teach them to deprive themselves or always put themselves "second"—but to teach them, simply, to share their bounty. It isn't always going to be easy to do this, but it is something that, with conditioning, will make our children's lives more joyful, and more fruitful. This is not the paradox it seems at first: It makes sense. We don't do good things in order for good things to be done to us, but the good things that will be done for us are a nice ancillary benefit.

A random act of kindness is just that: It's doing something for the world, or an individual in the world, with no expectation of thanks or reward. If you see litter, pick it up. It's not that you have to—you just want to. You can pay the highway toll for the person behind you, then speed away. You can leave a great book on the table at a restaurant for a stranger to enjoy. Ultimately, you will get this gift back a hundredfold—or someone else will, which is even better.

It doesn't always happen automatically, and you can give this process a little shove. For me, the philosophy called "Pay It Forward" is the easiest way to explain this "shove." Instead of "paying back" or getting paid back, you pay it *forward*. You can teach this principle to your children this way: When they do something for someone else, such as help a friend with their homework, they can ask in return for that kid to repay the act of kindness to *someone else*, or to multiple people, thus spreading the good through society exponentially. Although the phrase "pay it forward" was popularized by the science fiction writer Robert Heinlein in his book *Between Planets*, the concept is actually much older, dating back to 1784.

In 2006, Oprah did a "Pay It Forward" campaign by giving hundreds of her audience members $1,000 to give away to a stranger, and record the deed on a camcorder. The result was a tear-jerker.

When you and your children start to pay it forward, they start a chain reaction that begins in their life and touches countless others.

Love Isn't Real Unless You Give It Away

Giving of ourselves this way is not always easy. It sometimes might seem that when we're working to improve the lives of others, we're ignoring our own needs, and letting our own life fall by the wayside. This seems to make sense, but there are several serious flaws in thinking this way. We need to show our children that love is only real when we give it away to those around us, or even those who are far away. I've used this example before, and I will use it again. You love your children and give to them 24/7 not because you expect something in return for them. You love them because you receive joy from the loving, from seeing them grow and thrive and mature. Parenting is all about paying it forward. If you're really, really blessed, you do get "paid back" by your children much later, when they express their thanks for all you did. But in the meantime, all you need is a smile. That's *all it takes* to give you that joy and love back, many times multiplied!

I'm just thinking that it works the other way around, too: My father was away in Korea, where he'd been stationed in the air force for most of my childhood. But when I was ten, he came back. He was a military man, through and through, and very straight. If my father walked by and just flicked your nose, it was all the love you would need for weeks, and you could melt. Before he came home permanently, we saw him maybe once or twice a year. We'd see his uniform hanging in the hall, with the stripes. We'd smell his Old Spice, and we'd run into the bedroom to greet him (sometimes the timing was bad!).

I know he thought that same way about seeing me and my brother Andre grow. When he first saw us walking, or the first seconds of our first successful bike rides. That's all it takes.

This is probably all very obvious to you if you're a parent, but I'm stressing it to remind you about the reciprocal nature of giving.

That's the whole point of this book, isn't it? You are reading this book because you want your children to reach their dreams. You are aligning yourself with your children in order for them to succeed and have a beautiful life. Yet why do we so often resist giving to those around us, and therefore miss out on an opportunity to teach our children to do the same?

Well, for one thing, American culture and Western culture in general encourage individual growth and advancement. That's kind of the backbone of our capitalist economy and our ethic. Now, I don't think individualism and capitalism are bad things. On the contrary, we should encourage and cultivate that famous American "rugged individuality." I'm just saying it might help our society's ills if we raise positive, strong, freethinking children who don't think only about themselves. A purely self-serving, selfish path is not a path to achieving a dream. I believe wholeheartedly that we ought to raise children who are strong, balanced, and ambitious to achieve their dreams—while at the same time empathetic, loving, caring, and conscious of those around them. As parents, we can teach our children in one breath how important they are as people and, in the next breath, remind them that everyone else is *just as important.* It seems like a contradiction, but it's not.

How do you teach your children that we're all made of the same skin, bones, and other stuff? *You just tell them*, that's how. We're all coexisting in this Universe, and we're all remarkably similar. We all need food and shelter. We all need safety and security, and people who love us. We all want comfort. We all want to know that people care about our opinions. All of us share these simple wishes, but how many of us get caught up in attaining these things for ourselves, often at the expense of others? How simple it would be if we all started to encourage our children to befriend someone who doesn't have a lot of friends at school. How life-changing would it be if *your child* was the kid who no one sat with at lunch—and then someone sat with him? It would be *very* life-changing.

So I think we need to encourage our children to start making advancements in loving those around them—or at least thinking of their feelings, at least respecting them.

From No Man Is an Island:

There is a false and momentary happiness in self-satisfaction, but it always leads to sorrow because it narrows and deadens our spirit. True happiness is found in unselfish love, a love which increases in proportion as it is shared. There is no end to the sharing of love, and, therefore, the potential happiness of such love is without limit.

—Thomas Merton, 1955

~

What Exactly Is "Good"?

What happens when our children display selfishness? What happens when their single-minded journey toward dreams causes them to drive over the feelings of others?

First, we need to recognize that self-centeredness is a core phase in growing up. It's not unnatural, but it should be kept in check. We all have self-seeking desires, and we all sometimes step on other people's toes. We all think bad thoughts sometimes. It is natural and normal for your children not to be saints all the time. We can't set up impossible standards for our children. But we can foster an honest environment where we can speak with our children about others—their feelings, their desires, their needs, and their wants—and encourage them to consider others as they would themselves, or *at least* a close second. If our children act out unkindly to others, we need to be patient with them. Most of the time, our children's anger and occasional tendencies toward hurtful actions stem from something internal, not external. If such behavior becomes a pattern, it's worth exploring whether some inner wound is spurring our children to feel that they need to lash out, to get back at the world. Such feelings, though perfectly natural, can become disastrous if never confronted, if left to fester. They can prevent real growth and happiness, not to mention hurt others. Similarly, unkind thoughts or actions that are self-directed are equally important to nip in the bud. I am not saying that you should make your children feel guilty for feeling negative thoughts toward others. That wouldn't be fair because we *all* know those feelings so well (especially if you drive on the California freeway system!).

But it's certainly beneficial for you to communicate with your children about the source of their hurt: Why are they feeling hate, frustration, or pain? Our children are certainly entitled to their feelings—it's a natural part of growing up and getting to know themselves—but they're also deserving of the counsel that healing is better than hurting; loving is better than hating. If it is just a grumpy mood, fine! It will pass. But if you uncover a deeper, ongoing pain, anger, or even more serious psychological disturbance that's keeping your children from empathizing with others, then you have an emergent situation. You and the rest of your family can work on creating a loving, nurturing, and safe home environment that will move your children toward loving themselves, and therefore being able to love others. In the worst-case scenario, there's a lot of help out there in the form of child psychologists and counselors. Open yourself to their expertise.

Why Should We Do Good?

So why should we encourage our children to do good in the first place? Aren't we just trying to help them reach *their* goals, and not the goals of others? Why spread your time and energy thin thinking about other people's needs? After all, there are a lot of other people, with a lot of needs! There are all legitimate questions. But I think the question really should be, "Why do we *feel the need* to do good?" This, to me, better suits the discussion, because deep down, when we don't help people, when we pass the homeless woman on the side of the street and our children ask, "Mommy, why is that lady sleeping under the awning of that church?" we need to be ready to deal with the real feelings this brings up. If you say, "You know, we really ought to help her," you must be prepared to answer the next question, "Why? What's she got to do with us?"

The answer is an interesting one. But behind it is perhaps one of the most commonly overlooked tendencies in the human race. We feel some type of need to help those around us. When we don't, we feel bad. We feel "guilty." In general, I think guilt is a useless emotion, or worse—a counterproductive one—I've been trying to convince Ian of this since I met him. When you feel guilty because you were a bad boy twenty years ago, that's really not doing anyone, yourself included, any good. But the kind of guilt I'm talking about here is different. This kind of guilt is a message from the Universe that all is not right, that you're not playing your part, that you're not answering some natural, human call. We're all in this together, and no man is an island.

I'm not saying that you should answer the inquisitive child above with, "We should help that lady because otherwise we'll feel guilty." **Instead, I mean we should explore what our hearts and minds and souls are telling us about those in need, and we should help our children dig into that part of themselves; we must show them healthy ways to express their natural tendency toward giving, toward loving, toward others.**

Why Do Bad Things Happen to Good People? Why Do Some People Do Bad Things?

These are tough question to ask, and even tougher to answer when your children ask them. Without a doubt, they're questions that your children will ask you eventually. And even if they don't, you can consider starting the conversation in an age-appropriate way. There are several ways to go about discussing these sensitive issues:

1. Not everyone in the world has the same view of "good" that our family has. This might mean that people who have had some sort of hurt in their past don't feel like they are able to do good to those around them. Therefore, a person like this might hurt a person, an "innocent bystander" who really just wants to do good to others. If this were to happen to you, you'd be a good person

to whom a bad thing happened. But if you take apart what really happened, you'll find that what happened to you doesn't make *you* bad, and it doesn't even make the person who hurt you bad. If a bad thing happens to you, remember it's just a thing that happened to you— it's not *you*. You're still good. You didn't deserve what happened to you, but sometimes these things happen. You can choose to hold onto hurt and hate, but that will feed a monster inside you that won't leave much room for the good stuff, like fun and happiness. Or you can choose to forgive what happened to you. Why not? That way, you can move on with the rest of your day and your life.

2. As people, we all stray sometimes from what the Native Americans call "The Good, Red Road": the road of balance, right-living, and good conscience. Children and adults both stray. Sometimes we unintentionally hurt other people who didn't deserve to be treated that way. It's normal, but we have to try not to do it. When we do it, we need to apologize, and try to make up for our hurting someone. Not to live in guilt and shame about it, but to be honest about it, sorry for it, willing to make up for it, then ready to move on.

Sometimes people cause hurt even when they don't mean to be hurtful. They're just so caught up in their own pain that they're almost blind to everyone else. Obviously, this is not an enviable position. These people aren't bad people—but it would be much better for everyone if they healed themselves and stopped doing bad things. One thing they might consider trying is to do good to others, which would probably make them feel better and also help the other people. Or maybe they need to forgive themselves for something they did, because if they felt better about themselves, they might treat everyone else better. Maybe it would be easier for them to forgive themselves if *we* forgave them first.

3. Sometimes, there are just some things that go unexplained. Why do people become homeless? Why do dogs get hit by cars? Why do people who are born in certain parts of the world have to deal with AIDS and slavery and hunger and war? Why do good, honest, caring, loving people suffer? Why do children sometimes get very sick, and even die? Because things happen. Because God or nature or evolution or some other great force intends for that to happen. We have no control over certain things. But we can control what we do, and how we treat others.

A Very Good Boy

Ultimately, "good" and "bad" are in the mind. They're a matter of perspective. One person's hardship might be another person's awesome opportunity. Just go and take a look at *www.mattieonline.com*. That's the personal website of Mattie Stepanek, a young boy who had a rare form of muscular dystrophy called Dysautonomic Mitochondrial Myopathy. Mattie's physical disease was so severe that he needed a wheelchair to get around, and he had lots of trouble breathing on his own. Doctors told him he wouldn't have to wait long to be out of misery, as his life span would be short. But

Mattie wasn't one to sit around feeling sorry for himself. He decided he was put on Earth for a reason. He decided that everything about him—including his disease—had a purpose, and he undertook to discover it in the short time he had. Mattie turned what would have been unendurable pain and sadness in another into such a hopeful, loving, peaceful message of giving, that it's hard to even write about him without choking up (I'm telling you—check out that website!). Mattie's poetry books became *New York Times* bestsellers, and by the time of his death in 2004 at age thirteen, he had transformed the lives of millions who heard his hopeful story.

Mattie was twelve when he published his poems. He really paid it forward. His books are Dream Catchers of the highest order. Read them, and read them to your children. It's all they need to know about doing good in the world during our stay here.

Dream Catcher Eight

Be You

Believe in yourself. Stay in your own lane.
There's only one you.

—Entertainer Queen Latifah, summing up her mother's best advice
(*Reader's Digest*, October, 2008)

Y ou already know that your child is the only one of his
or her special kind out there, but here we will empha-
size the importance of that concept. As you strive to help
your children better themselves, it helps to be reminded to
counsel them: *Be the best* you *that you can be—because you
can't be anyone else.* In other words, your children can have
models, yourself included, but each child is unique, and
therefore must focus on his or her distinctive characteris-
tics. As parents, we need to encourage our children to imagine doing what they love to do every day (such as playing
lacrosse or bug-hunting) and building a life in which they
can do whatever they want *all of the time.* **When your children find the special talent that only they possess, great**

joy, abundance, prosperity, and peace will follow them all of their days.

The Road Less Traveled

At the core of each child is a strikingly unique person. People bandy that word *unique* around a lot, but it has real meaning behind the cliché: *Unique* means one-of-a-kind. And that's pretty miraculous considering there are 6.8 billion of us, and billions more who have passed before, and will come long after we're gone. Each utterly unique. The most essential thing about us is our novelty, our uniqueness. Yet we live in a world that constantly demands we conform. It's an astonishing paradox if you really think about it.

There's a great scene in the Peter Weir–directed movie *Dead Poets Society*: Robin Williams plays an unconventional teacher, John Keating, who takes his students into the stone courtyard of the school and asks a few of them to walk in a circle. Within seconds, the boys fall into line and begin marching in rhythm as the rest of the class claps to keep time. Keating has demonstrated his point. "Boys, you must strive to find your *own* voice. Because the longer you wait to begin, the less likely you are to find it at all. Thoreau said, 'Most men lead lives of quiet desperation' [*Walden*]. Don't be resigned to that. Break out!"

This whole time, an older teacher, Mr. McAllister, has been watching from a high window, disturbed at this dangerous lesson. Shouldn't it all be about conformity? Isn't that why we have schools, rules, laws? Without marching, don't we have chaos?

"Now we all have a great need for acceptance," Keating tells his students. "But you must trust that your beliefs are unique, your own, even though others may think them odd or unpopular, even though the herd may go, 'that's *baaaaad*.'"

Keating quotes a great American poet, Robert Frost, to solidify his point. In "The Road Not Taken" Frost writes, "Two roads diverged in the wood and I— / I took the one less traveled by, / and that has made all the difference."

Let that be the difference in the lives of your children. Let them take the un-trodden path, even if it be a path of some resistance. To paraphrase Thoreau's *Walden* again, let them put to rout all that was not life; and not, when they come to die, discover that they have not lived.

Fostering Individuality

The world can throw up resistance to children who are confident in their unique view, who know where they want their lives to go. Children who don't feel the desire to live as followers of the masses tend to threaten the majority. Those caught up in the masses believe that conformity is key to living a happy, problem-free life (actually, they're just hiding out, hoping no one will notice that they *are* different). But what kind of life is it, trying to emulate everyone else? It's like living in a hall of mirrors, where you eventually can't tell which "you" is really *you*. We need to help our children smash as many of those mirrors as they can, and to look *inward* for true reflection. How can we encourage such audacious individuality?

DISCOURAGE CONFORMITY

When I was growing up, I didn't want to be a kind of farm animal, living in a pen, getting milked by one of those machines. In some ways, my parents, though they meant well, didn't understand that mentality, and always struggled to give me that dose of "reality." You know the script: *Do well in school, go to college, get a good-paying, "normal" job.* That's not bad advice in general—except it just wasn't me. I tried, I really did, but I'm thankful the true me was able to break out of that mold. I really didn't want to have to conform to someone else's idea of what I should be. I didn't want to have to constantly answer that question that comes from the outside forces, "Are you *worthy?*" Based on what? Your application criteria? Your syllabus and policies and procedures? Your job description? I didn't want someone else choosing me because I was *their* idea of good or right.

I wanted to *be* the chooser, for myself. Because even if I *did* get chosen by "them," I didn't want that to be the thing that made me feel "worthy." Don't get me wrong. You and your children do need others sometimes. You do need acceptance (to schools, jobs, programs, contests, etc.). They'll lock you up if you stand on the Olympic podium with a handmade medal and declare yourself the best high-jumper in the world.

I'm just saying it's best not to let those outside approvals or disapprovals define *who you are.* When your decision to define yourself is taken from you, you've lost your identity.

You've lost it all. I knew a guy in L.A. who was CEO of a huge company, and lost his job when the economy tanked. You know what he did? He took his own life. He couldn't live with the idea of *not* being CEO. But what you *do* is not *who you are*, so there's really no point in just doing what everyone else does. It's easier to teach this vital lesson to our children when they're young, and not yet filled and influenced by multiple years of external inputs about their "worthiness," as defined by how closely they can mimic everyone else.

DESTROY SHAME

Shame poisons individuality and kills uniqueness. From a young age, don't allow shame in your household. You can criticize, you can guide, you can make it clear that certain behaviors are not right—but avoid using the "Shame-on-you" school of behavior-correction. Shame goes to the person, not their actions. It says, "*You* are bad." I think it is because I worked hard to keep shame out of my household that Raven and Blaize have such strong senses of self, and such powerful individuality. What I see in Raven as an adult that makes me proud is that she's a respectful, wise young woman who's not ashamed of what she wants—and has no reason to be. She's self-possessed. She handles herself well and reveals herself to the world in a positive way.

Be Yourself Even When It's Hard

I remember once when we were doing *Cosby*, we came home to be with family in Atlanta for the holidays. Raven was on a local news channel, WXIA-TV, "11 Alive." I was just offscreen watching her interview with the anchor when a spot came on the monitors. People were talking about the downside of Christmas, and especially how crime tends to go up during the holidays. Well, all they showed in this video were black people. And then there was a commercial, and this one was all about the wonderful parts of Christmas—you know, family, turkey, presents, Santa. And this commercial showed only white people. The anchor and I—she was African American— just looked at each other, and shook our heads. Then we looked at Raven. I'm not trying to make this a black-white thing. I'm just talking about shame and self-image. How easy would it be considering the constant barrage of those images, for a child to just start incorporating shame and self-loathing into her sense of self? I mean all kids who don't fit the "mold." Thankfully, Raven never succumbed to shame—because we countered those messages with our own, and we out-shouted them!

Along these lines, once Bill Cosby told me that when he first pitched his show idea, some bigwigs wanted to make his character, Cliff Huxtable, a limo driver instead of a doctor. The network people thought America wasn't ready to deal with blacks in that kind of role. Yikes.

I like to think I helped Raven understand that she could play beautiful, talented, and articulate characters, and she could represent such qualities in her real life, too. When you decide to be *you*, you deny the way others try to define you. Eventually they will give up trying and let you be you. We sent Raven that message, and Raven's still there in the right frame of mind. She's not trying to mirror other people's attitudes about the way she should look or act or believe. You don't see her taking on stereotypical roles (like the "neck-twistin' sassy black chick") that the media so often portrays. And you don't see her in uncompromising positions on websites—even though that's worked wonders for some celebrities' careers.

~

CULTIVATE CHARACTER

Now there's a word from the old days that we need to resurrect. I know my friend Bill Cosby would agree. *Character* is our ability to recognize right from wrong; it's the inner voice that doesn't judge, but guides us in the right direction; it's the ability to empathize with other people's feelings; it's our will to kindness and gentleness; and it's our consistency and our work ethic and our unshakable belief in ourselves and what we can achieve. This is who you are, and this predicts how happy you will be, and how likely you will be to get to your dreams.

Raven was just "being herself" when she turned to me and Lydia and announced her dream. The character is set when we are very young, and we had fostered in her a strong one, one that had her believing there was nothing she couldn't do. Part of character is an inner sense that you are special, you are unique, you are amazing. Alexander the Great's mother used to tell him he was born of Zeus and akin to Achilles; that he would one day rule the world. It was a stretch, but damn—he pretty much did it! That's what happens when you actually name your kid "the Great." Imagine what the world might have been like had Olympias and King Philip named him Alexander the Mediocre or Alex the Blah.

TEACH YOUR CHILDREN SELF-RELIANCE

Remind them: Because you're the only you among the 6.8 billion, no one else will ever care quite as much as you about your dream. All those other people are kind of busy with their own stuff. Even your parents can't care as much as you do. I could name you Alexander "the Great," I could give you Aristotle as a tutor, and I can tell you that you'll rule the world someday. But *you* have to at some point get on a horse and take up a bow and arrow, and head out to spread the Greek way of life to the East. It's all on you. This is as true today as it was in the fourth century B.C.E.: People aren't likely to knock down your door when you're just at home admiring yourself in the mirror, calling yourself "the Great."

CELEBRATE YOUR CHILDREN'S SPECIAL QUALITIES

Don't stifle your children's eccentricity or squash their quirks. The quirks are what make them *them*, what separates them from the 6.8 billion other people. Raven happened to know what she wanted from when she was young, but we were also aware of something deeply special about her before she could even talk. As a parent, I'm sure that you've experienced that same sensation. You're aware of that flare in your child. Watch and listen for it, and when you see it, fan it, flame it, and your child will ignite the world.

COUNTER THE CONFORMISTS

When your children start to go to school, be on guard for the negative comments that are bound to come their way. Be alert about their freedom being hampered. We all encounter people who want to discourage creativity and individuality. We all deal with institutions where convention reigns supreme. Traditionalism. Compliance. Obedience. Submission. We have to teach our children to rebel to some extent against these prevailing orthodoxies. Sure, we don't want our children leaping out the windows of school, naked and singing "I've Gotta Be Me" like Sammy Davis, Jr., every time there's a standardized test. But nor do we want them to give up their freedom to be themselves. We don't want them to turn into mindless automatons. Robots programmed by the powers that be to perform certain tasks at their command, and never break protocol.

ALLOW SELF-EXPLORATION

Give your children space to discover who they are. Children get to mold themselves, though you can act as a kind of art director, supervising that sculpture. All of us have to survey the world, and delve into areas that make us feel alive, that make us feel like *us*. Don't discourage this adventurous spirit in your children, even if they sometimes go to places you might not have gone, or you have yet to explore. Give them a flashlight, a helmet, and a strong line tied around their waist—then let them go spelunking!

ENCOURAGE AN ADVENTUROUS SPIRIT — WITHIN REASON

Just because you give your children a long leash with which to discover themselves does not mean you should condone your children getting into bad stuff or hanging around a bad scene. In fact, those experiences tend to encourage conformity, not individuality, which irony you can explain to your children, and show them. Act not as a gatekeeper to these situations, but more as a safe counsel for your children to talk with, to ask advice, to seek support.

PARTICIPATE

Actively help your child's distinctive character blossom. Be weird and goofy with your kid! "Gaiety is wiser than wisdom," according to historian Will Durant. So have fun with your children, let their freak flag fly! If you are comfortable with who they are, they will feel more comfortable with who they are.

Getting Out of the Box

We learn when we're little children that no two snowflakes are exactly alike, and we seize on this idea. We love it. Then we spend the rest of our childhoods trying to be exactly like everyone else. Euripides, one of the greatest authors of the Greek tragedies, writes, "There is just one life for each of us: our own." This has been something I have always thought about while we were raising Raven and Blaize. As our children get older, this fear of individuality rears its head. When children are young, they run through the house singing songs and acting silly. They're not concerned with their appearance or what others think of them. When they start going to school, though, many want to be "a part of the crowd," rather than an individual. Individuals stick out. So they allow the conformity of the crowd to rain down on them, snuff out that light that's inside them—and sometimes it's hard to get that spark going again.

As soon as our children begin to imitate other people for the sake of fitting in, they forfeit their own dreams for a second-rate version of someone else's dream. Our children are meant to be inimitable, original works of art, not copies. But this desire to be someone else stems from a deep insecurity about the validity of their own dreams. So we parents need to create an environment that enables our children to feel comfortable with who they are and prepares them to enter that harshly conformist social world with a strong, healthy ego and a willingness to persevere.

When children have the courage to express themselves, that courage might sometimes come at the expense of being accepted by their peers. While at first this might seem like a harsh negative, I see it differently, as a clear sign of a strong and healthy *individual*. This is good! Children at all times need to know that they *must follow their own voices.* Every child comes into this world with a special dream, with particular talents and wishes that *no one else possesses* in the same measure. So why would we urge them to suppress that individualism in favor of blending in? Look, as parents you understand that you can't please everyone all the time, so you need to explain this reality to your children as soon as they can grasp the concept. Show your children examples of historical figures who followed their own expression and didn't cave in to the pressure to be one of the herd. Or show them that their heroes from movies so often have to stick to their guns, even when everyone around them seems to be against them. If your children's self-expression is positive and productive and causing no one any harm, you should encourage it, always, and never advise them to bend to the will of the masses just to make life easier. The power of these Dream Catchers along with a strong family support system will help your children weather the storms that will inevitably blow their way as a result of their individuality.

~

Finding Myself Helped Me Help My Children Find Themselves

In 1976, when I was sixteen, I was driving a powder-blue 1966 Mustang and I was *the man.* But it hadn't been easy to get there—and it wouldn't last forever.

I had entered high school in Decatur after we left first Connecticut then Atlanta, feeling like I had to start all over again making a name for myself, and making new friends.

It was particularly hard for me, because my brother, Andre, had just left for college. I hated this limbo state at first, but I used two weapons to conquer my discomfort: music, and comedy. I loved diving and tennis, but for some reason, my mother elbowed me toward the band. The conductor made me first clarinet, which means I was pretty good, and I even got private lessons (it was a very suburban life, I see now). I think my mother must have somehow seen music in me, even before I did, because she turned out to be right: The band was the right place for me to discover my dreams.

Yes, the band was also full of nerds, but somehow I fit in easily there, and found friends. I made everybody laugh their asses off, so other non-band friends came easily too.

In fact, I had begun to hang out more frequently with a rougher gang of kids. For a while there, the principal and I had a very special relationship, and saw each other a lot. Actually, his paddle saw my butt a lot! Academically, I was a pretty solid "B" student, so everyone knew I wasn't likely to turn a corner and start robbing liquor stores.

Because my mother was a schoolteacher, bringing home a "C" would have been met with extreme retribution (you can imagine the nightmare that parent-teacher conferences were with a teacher and a military man as parents!). My problem was mainly that I sometimes acted the fool, and talked too much in school, and got busted for it all the time. I was a smooth operator, though, and often was able to charm my way out of trouble.

Traveling with the concert band was one of the best experiences of my youth. I loved it—especially the attention from the girlies, who loved my giant 'fro. All kidding aside, though,

I found that music was a great passion. I felt I understood it somehow, and it understood me. I started to pay close attention to the feelings it gave me, I believed in my abilities, and I knew I would stick with it throughout my life. Music moved me, literally.

So when I was sixteen, I founded a dance group with some other guys from the band. We were called the Derby Gang. The most popular dance craze in the Atlanta area was called the "bubblegum," and it was culturally huge at the time. The Jackson 5 were the biggest teen idols in history, already the granddaddies of the black bubblegum movement that's still spawning soundalikes to this day. And we could dance to the J-5 like nobody's business. We really made that dance our own. It was hard to do, and we could do it well, so the Derby Gang quickly became the group other guys wanted to get in. It's a great feeling to be the guy other guys want to be like, instead of the other way around. There were challenges between rival groups, with red lights and blaring stereos, where all the groups had to "turn it out" in front of an audience of mostly screaming girls. (To picture the bubblegum, you have to imagine a precursor to pop-locking, a smoother, less jerky version of that.)

There were *five* of us guys, of course, and we got good enough to do talent shows around the city. That helped me pop in school, because people in the hallways recognized me. And then we hit big: We got on a local Atlanta TV show called *Future Shock* on WTCG-TV Channel 17. It was basically our local *American Bandstand* or *Soul Train*, and it was on every Friday night. Best of all, it was hosted by the hardest working man in show business, *the* Mr. James Brown.

Although I was pretty popular at this point, at the top of my high school game, I still *really* wanted to fit in. All kids do. Well, I can tell you that in 1977, standing on stage with James Brown on one of the city's most popular shows had a tendency to make one look pretty fly with the guys and the ladies.

After that, the Derby Gang got bookings all over the place, and wherever we went, people cheered like we were the Beatles. At least it felt like that! At the time, I was having fun and hanging out with friends. You know, finding my niche. When I was performing, I didn't have a care in the world, which is how I knew I was in the right place, I was in the "zone." But without realizing it, I was also training as a performer and a manager. I was learning about being on the road, and dealing with egos. I was training for my future life.

And on my own a lot more, I was also getting what my mother would call more "rowdy." I even started to smoke, like Richard Roundtree in *Shaft*.

It wasn't long before my newfound "fame" and "fortune" (I was "working at the car wash" for my first real job) led me to desire more . . . let's say, *freedom* from my parents. I wanted to stay out later, they said no, I sneaked out, they caught me, I got punished, I rebelled even more . . . you've heard this story before, it's a complete cliché. But at the time, of course, it felt like life or death. Suffice to say my new attitude met with *great resistance* from my parents. I mean, *wow*, it was very explosive.

But I'm so glad it all happened. This conflict, this constant questioning of my boundaries and my way of life—this growing up—all set the stage for my awakening in that basement room at age seventeen. And it would set me up to be a parent myself eight short years later.

I think back on those Derby Gang years now because I hope it will be instructive for parents in that *if-I-knew-then-what-I-know-now* kind of way. There are two important messages to be found here, each having to do with being yourself.

Conflict Is Inevitable

There is going to be conflict as you form a sense of "you." Period. And it can often be useful. Conflict *wakes you up*. It forces you into another direction. If everything's going smoothly, you might tend to stay for the sake of the status quo. But as soon as you see a wall in front of you, you're forced to think, "I've got to find another way." And the moment you do that, bricks will fall away, or a ladder will appear, or a window will open, and you'll find that other way.

I'm not saying that you should go out of your way to *choose* discomfort, or *create* conflict with your children. Conflict will come on its own, rest assured, because conflict is nature. You can't forge metal without sparks. But when your children find themselves in a conflicted situation—a new school, an important choice, a fight over "rights"—you can assure them that it's okay to feel conflicted, and show them how to use that conflict to their advantage, to ask for and to seek ways through it, and not to turn tail. This is the difference between those children who succeed and find happiness, and those who flounder and fall into misery or mediocrity.

It's up to you to teach your children that "conflict" makes us stronger. That it bubbles our convictions up and boils them over the top. It makes us much *more* certain, never less, of who we are, and what we believe.

That is, if we don't run from it. If we don't cower. If we don't surrender. So my advice is to impress upon your kids to never give in! Tell them all about those times in your past that you thought it would be impossible, that you couldn't see a way out, that you were an inch from defeat, but overcame. Our entire nation was founded on such principles. Just listen to our national anthem: A glimpse of the tattered stars and stripes above the carnage of the battlefield was enough to keep the patriots going.

Or take your children outside on a clear night and look up. Explain to them that it was conflict that made the stars and galaxies. Raging, crashing, furious conflict. Without it, none of us would be here. Conflict literally forges us in the fires, shapes us in the collisions, situates us in the heavens. None of it is pretty or smooth or gentle. But it works. It's perfect.

Show your children that they don't have to take the so-called failure and the unavoidable troubles of life as something inherently negative. We grow through those conflicts. We make ourselves. Constantly come back to this concept of "growth" whenever you talk with your children about conflict. Remind them of the stories of all the most famous, wealthiest, most successful people in the world, who all crashed into "failure" multiple times. Henry Ford. Thomas Edison. Abraham Lincoln. The Wright Brothers after busting their asses falling out of the sky so many times. The masses at one time or another called all these people crazy. People begged Rosa Parks not to sit at the front of the bus. People told Gandhi to shut up live under British rule.

Becoming you sometimes sucks, and often hurts. What you don't want to do, as you help your children create themselves, is pretend that life is always sweet and neat and gleeful, that nobody fights, that people don't get angry, that bad stuff—even really bad stuff—never happens. This seems to be the inclination of many new parents. I suppose they're just so afraid of "hurting" their children that they wish to protect them from all the evils of the world, to build a kind of fairyland force field around their children's lives. I understand that. Of course there was nothing I wouldn't have done to protect my kids—I'd have taken a bullet for them. I still would. But we're not talking about taking bullets. We're talking about taking away chances to feel, to experience, to grow up, to become whole. We're talking about "protecting" our children from life. From truth. And that can't be a good thing.

——————— BEING YOU SOMETIMES HURTS ———————

When I was in the seventh grade in Atlanta, I had a German Shepherd named King. He was almost pure white. One morning, I was across the street at the bus stop, and saw

King coming out of the house. Down the street a Pontiac was coming our way, fast. I shouted at King to stay, but he just bolted toward me, tail wagging, tongue flapping in the wind. He wanted to be with me. I can't write about what happened next, except to say I loved that dog, and it causes me pure pain when I think about it, even now. Despite my begging, my parents didn't let me come to the vet. They just took him away, and he never came back. They were trying to protect me.

Even when my grandparents died, my parents didn't let me go to the funerals. Again, the idea was to protect me, to save me from sadness, I guess. But I wonder about this logic now. It seems to me we need to properly prepare our children for an understanding of this kind of pain. I was trying to "be me" at those moments—part of me was devastated, and I needed to express it.

Look, of course as a parent you will always maintain the authority to choose what you share with your children, and when to share it. And naturally these decisions must be made based on age-appropriateness and taking into account the maturity and readiness of your child. All I'm saying is that children can experience the full range and panoply of human emotions—it's part of them. It *is* them. So as they explore ways to be themselves, they're going to go through some difficult emotional stuff. It isn't always our job to "save" them from that—it's to help them through it, and guide them through appropriate and healthy expressions.

Teaching Raven to Roll With It

Along these lines, I hope you don't misunderstand me when I talk about Raven's meteoric rise to success—it wasn't always easy for her, either. You have to remember, she was still just a young girl when big things started to happen. And as a very young actress, she had to overcome doubts from others about her lack of acting experience. Later, she had to overcome concerns that only a few young African-American girls had carried their own television shows. When she entered adolescence, there were questions about her weight and, just like other teenagers, she struggled with peer problems. I remember once as she began middle school, the principal made an announcement on the PA: "Don't crowd around Raven-Symoné. Don't ask for her autograph, or you'll get detention." You can imagine how she wanted to crawl into the mop closet and hide.

There were slow times in Raven's acting and music careers, and she had to deal with people judging her about that as well. But she was able to remember that she was on a journey, and that her abilities had not changed regardless; it was okay to go through these things, and it was not the end of the world.

Another time, when Raven was thirteen, we were doing the *Undeniable* album when Stevie Wonder called. He said, "I loved that song you did, 'With a Child's Heart.' I just wrote a song for you, Raven. It's called 'I Love You.'" He wanted to do the track together, so he came to Baltimore as we were recording, and we spent three days together. Raven was in the booth trying to get the vocals perfect, but she was so nervous about letting Stevie down. At some point, Stevie's handlers left, and he asked me to take him into the other room so he could play the piano. I was anxious, too: I thought I might accidentally steer him into a wall and knock him out of tune! Poor Raven. She came of the booth, and started crying, saying, "Daddy." *I'd never seen her breaking down like that*, especially at work. I mean she'd met presidents, hung out with Michael Jackson, toured with 'N Sync. But this day, she said, "I can't do it. It's *Stevie Wonder*."

I said, "Do what? Baby, just *do you*. You'll be perfect." And I wiped her eyes, and she went back in the booth, and laid it down.

Through this process, I tried to be a positive role model. If parents are excessively harsh on themselves, pessimistic, or unrealistic about their abilities and limitations, their child might eventually mirror them. I wanted to set an example for my children by being positive and forgiving of myself.

But can you imagine how hard it was for Raven to deal with producers and directors turning her down for jobs as she got older because of her weight? Of course I wanted to shield her from these criticisms, and protect her from these pains, but how would that help her to keep becoming herself? Learning to deal with disparagement and shallow condemnation made Raven stronger, gave her a greater sense of herself, solidified her mold. And now she helps other young girls understand where body image really comes from, what healthy really means, and what self-esteem is all about.

How to Be the Best You That You Can Be

It's important to start helping your children feel more comfortable in their skin from a very early age. Try explaining it to your child this way: "You are the only person in the world that is like you. There is no one else that will ever be the same as you. Because you are so unique, you have something all your own that you can give to the world." By talking this way to your child, you will avoid the tragic possibility that your children will walk away from their true self to play some safer fictional role they're cast in by society. Show them: Why *play* a role when you can *be* the real thing?

Be You and Be Your Dreams

This last Dream Catcher insists that you teach your children to quiet their minds and listen to their souls. Sometimes you wonder where a thought comes from. *I just had this great idea*, you might say. Ideas seem to come out of nowhere. But where is "nowhere"? Ideas about who you are and what you want to accomplish don't come from nowhere. Instead, they come from some great source somewhere (maybe it's within you, or maybe it comes from a higher power—or maybe it's both). This source contains a vast storehouse of ideas, including the idea for our destiny.

And children are the same. They have what at first seems like an emptiness, from lack of experience and lack of complex thought, but they, too, have a *vast reserve*, with access to awesome potential. Even in the jungle, alone, a child will learn how to feed himself, clean himself, build a shelter. Even on a desert island, a child will grow to discover her own unique talents and interests. One might bang together coconuts and one might paint on the walls of a cave. A child will dream, and look for ways to achieve her dream. And your child is not alone in the jungle, nor stranded on a desert island. Teachers and coaches and friends and patrons will come and go. Some might be greatly influential. Some might be fleeting. But as a parent, you will always be there. So you will *always* be able to help them.

So the key is to help your child unlock this code, uncover this destiny, unfurl his or her soul's purpose like a personal flag. "Who's the special 'you' inside?" you can ask. "Everyone is different, and everyone has a different purpose and dream. What's yours?"

Conclusion

Get Going!

*At bottom every man knows well enough that he
is a unique being, only once on this earth; and by
no extraordinary chance will such a marvelously
picturesque piece of diversity in unity as he is, ever be
put together a second time.*

—Friedrich Nietzsche, nineteenth-century German philosopher

Y ou might be wondering just how long it will take for
your children to find real success. Well, if you want to
be very, very good at some special skill such as banjo-playing
or shipbuilding, then surprisingly, there's actually a specific
answer to that question. Social anthropologist Malcolm
Gladwell culled together years of research on the subject and
answers the question in his book *Outliers*. Researchers studying the wildly successful—those virtuoso talents at the pinna-
cle of their fields, whether they be hockey players, musicians,
scientists, or computer programmers—have determined
that such proficiency does not come cheap in terms of time
investment. In fact, on average, these people spend about

10,000 hours practicing and apprenticing *before* they get good enough for the designation "star." Ten thousand hours. That's ten hours a week for a thousand weeks (nearly twenty years). Or more like fifty hours a week for 200 weeks (less than four years). However you calculate, though, one thing is clear—major success does not come to the hobbyist or the dabbler. You have to dedicate yourself entirely to get the big rewards. This 10,000-hours number keeps coming up in the research. It's how much time Bill Gates spent programming before he *started* Microsoft. It's how much time U.S. Olympic fencer Jason Rogers trained (ten years of five-hour training days) before his first Olympics in Athens in 2004—and Rogers was trounced in less than five minutes (then had to spend thousands *more* hours practicing and consulting with a sports psychologist before he could win a silver medal in the 2008 games in Beijing).

Let the Dream-Catcher Journey Commence Today

Your children have come here to be themselves. To do a specific thing, to fulfill a certain mission. Your children have come here to dream big—and to achieve their dreams. You must encourage them to do that which brings them joy and makes them feel complete. Not for Mommy and Daddy, not for the money, or the fame, or the glory—but for themselves.

Here's how you can explain it to them: You have a limited time in this life, between zero and "unspecified." You came into this life with nothing, and you'll leave with nothing, as far as we know. So in between you're supposed to create what you love, and love what you create. That's it.

You get to choose happiness or not. You get to achieve your dream or not. No matter what happens around you— *you* get to decide. As long as you're constantly moving forward toward that happiness, you're getting closer to fulfilling that dream. So fill your finite time with the pursuit of your desires. The time will pass anyway. So you might as well go for your dreams. And I'll help you every step of the way.

References

Baldwin, James. *Nobody Knows My Name: More Notes of a Native Son.* New York: Dial Press, 1961.

Brooks, Arthur C. *Gross National Happiness: Why Happiness Matters for America—And How We Can Get More of It.* New York: Basic Books, 2008.

Byrne, Rhonda. *The Secret.* New York: Atria Books, 2006.

Delcourt, Marcia A. B. *What Parents Need To Know about . . . Recognizing Interests, Strengths, and Talents of Gifted Adolescents.* Storrs, CT: National Research Center on the Gifted and Talented, 1998.

Dyer, Wayne W. *The Power of Intention: Learning to Co-create Your World Your Way.* Carlsbad, CA: Hay House, 2004.

Frankl, Victor E. *Man's Search for Meaning: An Introduction to Logotherapy.* Translated by Ilse Lasch. Boston: Beacon, 2006.

Frost, Robert. *Selected Poems*. Edited and with an introduction by Ian Hamilton. Harmondsworth: Penguin, 1973.

Gladwell, Malcolm. *Outliers: The Story of Success*. New York: Little, Brown and Company, 2008.

Heinlein, Robert A. *Between Planets*. New York: Scribner, 1951.

Herbert, Frank. *Dune*. Philadelphia: Chilton Books, 1965.

James, William. "What Is an Emotion?" *Mind* 9 (1884): 188–205.

Johnson, Melissa. "First Step in Becoming a Winner: Act Like One." *New York Times*, March 20, 2009.

Lipton, Bruce H. *The Biology of Belief: Unleashing the Power of Consciousness, Matter, and Miracles*. Carlsbad, CA: Hay House, 2008.

Merton, Thomas. *No Man Is an Island*. New York: Harcourt, Brace, 1955.

Ruiz, Miguel. *The Four Agreements: A Practical Guide to Personal Freedom*. San Rafael, CA: Amber-Allen Publishing, 1997.

Scaglione, Robert, and William Cummins. *Karate of Okinawa: Building Warrior Spirit.* New York: Person-to-Person Publishing, Inc., 1990.

Schwartz, David J. *The Magic of Thinking Big.* Englewood Cliffs, NJ: Prentice Hall, 1959.

Thoreau, Henry David. *Walden.* Philadelphia, PA: Courage Books, 1990.

Acknowledgments

Christopher B. Pearman

First and foremost, I would like to thank the Universe, and the wonderful underlying vibration that animates all things. And I would like to thank the many wonderful people who have contributed so much along this journey:

I want to thank my mother and father, Dorothy and Joseph Pearman, for their boundless support and love. They are, and always have been, my inspiration, for they always made me want to be great at anything and everything I did. I love them for that.

I also would like to thank the mother of my children, Lydia, who contributed so much to this journey with her love, understanding, and support. There is no mother greater, no mother more honored and loved than Lydia.

Stephanie Austin from Atlanta Young Faces modeling agency. She was the first to believe in Raven and our family.

Bill Cosby is owed a great debt of thanks for taking a chance with Raven on his tremendously successful show, and for all his wisdom and insight in the business of show.

NBC for their wonderful support through the years.

David Brokaw of the Brokaw Company for his PR genius.

Norman Brokaw of the William Morris agency for his knowledge and friendship.

MCA Records for providing the opportunity to fulfill Raven's dreams of a recording career.

Mark Curry and the cast and crew of the *Hangin' with Mr. Cooper* show for a great run.

Eddie Murphy and the *Dr. Dolittle* franchise for Raven's first big movie experience.

The Walt Disney Company and their wonderful backing and belief in Raven.

Gary Marsh, President of Entertainment for the Disney Channel, Worldwide—the best television creative on the planet—for his wonderful friendship.

Adam Bonnet for being an angel.

Jamilla Anderson, the Nubian Princess.

Michael Poryes for his wonderful writing—his genius helped Raven reach the stars.

For my son, Blaize, I say thanks for being the wonderful angel that he is. He, too, is giving the world a beautiful gift, and I'm so proud of him.

My Nunu for believing in all that I do, and for inspiring me to write.

Aljai Wallace for starting me on my spiritual journey— without him this book would not exist.

Steve Carson for being the first agent that helped me get Raven on *The Cosby Show*. Steve, you'll always be the man.

Cindy Osbrink from the Osbrink Talent Agency for securing the *That's So Raven* project.

Valeria Arnold, VP of Rayblaize3Entertainment, my partner in my business life.

Thank you to my best friends, Dr. Vito Guarnaccia and his lovely wife, Elizabeth. I love you guys.

Trina, rest in peace, girl. We miss you!

For all of you who were there on this journey, I send you my love and appreciation.

Ian Blake Newhem

Christopher and I are grateful to our brilliant agent, Celeste Fine of Folio Literary Management, and to Chelsea King, Wendy Simard, and all the cool people at Adams Media for believing in Christopher's idea.

I thank David Newhem for his love and support of my dreams. You *are* my dream, Dave!

I thank Hannah and Ellanah Newman for daily living their dreams.

I thank Maris and Steve Newman for allowing me to pursue my dream of writing, and not pushing that lawyer thing too hard.

Finally, I thank Urban Eisen-Miller for his superb intellect and faithful assistance.

Index

About the Authors

Christopher B. Pearman

Christopher B. Pearman, fifty, studied political science and criminal justice at Georgia State before settling into a career in public relations and advertising. When his firstborn, Raven-Symoné, arrived in 1985, he was working in the evenings doing PR for the nightclub industry in Atlanta. This allowed him to stay home with baby Raven, where he almost immediately discovered her natural abilities and talents. Soon after Raven announced to her parents that she wanted to be on *The Cosby Show*, Pearman got to work managing her career. He continued in that role for more than two decades, and now remains a multifaceted entertainment industry player. He has produced and directed music videos, including Raven's "Supernatural" and "Superstition" videos, as well as several short films. He served as creative consultant for, and directed episodes of, the hit TV show *That's So Raven*, the Disney Channel's longest-running and highest-rated series, which starred his daughter, Raven-Symoné. He has coproduced and directed national TV commercials for the Hasbro Toy Company. He has appeared on *Live with Regis & Kathie Lee*, as well as dozens of other national TV and radio spots. He lives in Burbank, California, with his dogs, Drago and Jazz.

Ian Blake Newhem

Ian Blake Newhem, forty-one, is the coauthor and editor (as Ian Blake Newman) of *The 30-Day Diabetes Miracle* series (2007, 2008: Penguin-Perigee), as well as *Managing the College Newsroom* (2003: Associated Collegiate Press, International, Minneapolis, MN), in use at 700+ colleges and universities. He has placed in competitions and published more than 100 articles, stories, and essays in regional and national newspapers and magazines, including *Utne Reader*; the *North Dakota Quarterly; Writer's Digest; Story* magazine; the *Journal News* (a Gannett Suburban paper); the Middletown *Times Herald-Record* (an Ottaway paper); *Brain, Child*; *Genre*; and *Really*. He has been contributing editor at *Hudson Valley Magazine*, and has been twice nominated for a Pushcart Prize. Newhem has run his own writing and editing business, Blakerite Enterprises, since 1991. He does business writing for major clients, including *Fortune* 500 companies in the health, education, banking, construction, and real estate industries. Newhem is a tenured associate professor of literature, composition, and journalism in the honors program at the State University of New York, Rockland, where he has chaired both the English department and the Humanities, Behavioral & Social Sciences division. He has traveled extensively in the United States and abroad, lecturing on writing, journalism ethics, and lifestyle medicine, and judging national and international journalism and writing competitions. He has appeared on hundreds of TV and radio stations. He lives with his partner and his dogs, Max and T-bone, in upstate New York.

to lean on &
always there)) security

Mike Huckabee said "We r people leading us i n c country club but not Sams club. p n l golf score 2 last ink but n r price of eggs or milk. The only thing worse p l caring about people i are struggling & barely staying above H_2O is l even n. t there they're out there"

Parents r good intentions & want l (" parents bt perhaps n r forgotten or never r been taught or never experienced good parenting. Parents u often in a struggling frustrated situation s r want s need help but society has u prepared p r do so. We r r r. license r drive & r r so we r r r schooling s experience but parenting require none of this & yet r r r most r put u n earth